HEATHER ROSS
PRINTS

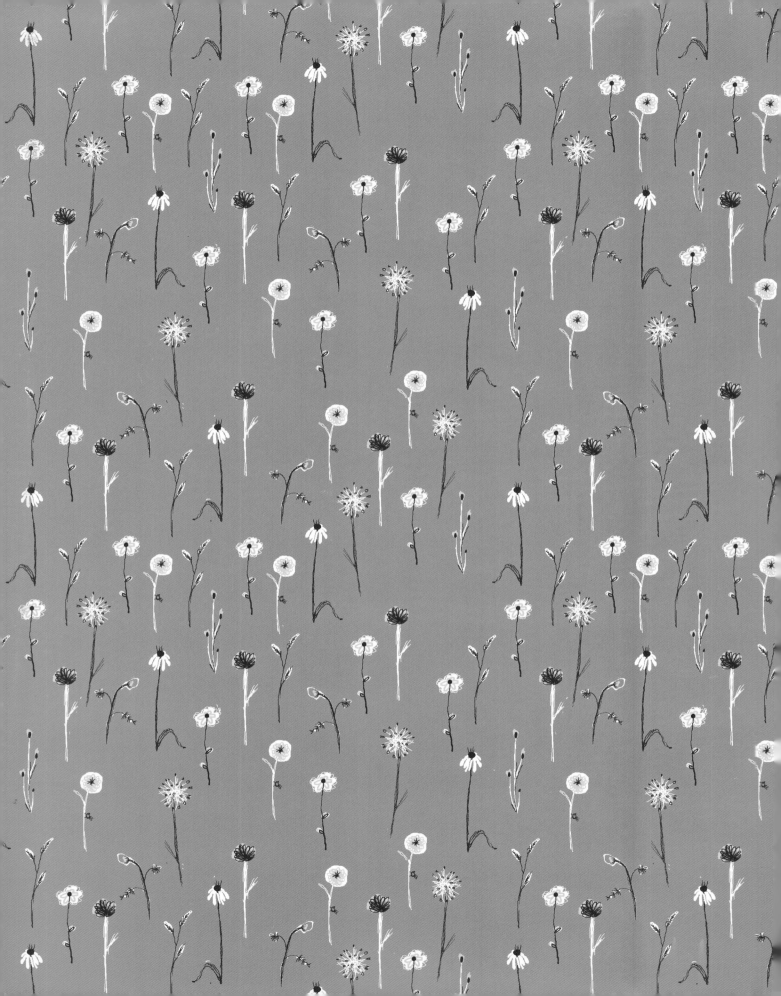

HEATHER ROSS
PRINTS

50+ DESIGNS AND 20 PROJECTS TO GET YOU STARTED

PHOTOGRAPHS BY JOHN GRUEN

STC CRAFT | A MELANIE FALICK BOOK | NEW YORK

Published in 2012 by Stewart, Tabori & Chang
An imprint of ABRAMS

Text and illustrations copyright © 2012 by Heather Ross
Photographs copyright © 2012 by John Gruen

Library of Congress Cataloging-in-Publication Data:
Ross, Heather.
Heather Ross prints / by Heather Ross.
p. cm.
"A Melanie Falick book."
Includes bibliographical references and index.
ISBN 978-1-58479-995-5
1. Textile printing. 2. Prints. 3. Paper products. I. Title.
TT852.R67 2012
746.6'2—dc23
2011053263

Editor: Liana Allday
Designer: Brooke Reynolds for inchmark
Production Manager: Tina Cameron

The text of this book was composed in Avenir.

Printed and bound in China.
10 9 8 7 6 5 4 3 2 1

THE ART OF BOOKS SINCE 1949

115 West 18th Street
New York, NY 10011
www.abramsbooks.com

For my mother,
Tess Beemer, who told me
that I should be an artist.

CONTENTS

INTRODUCTION

I first had the idea to create this book a few years ago when I was asked to speak at the New York Public Library about their rare books collection and its potential as a resource for artists, crafters, and fabric designers. The week before the event, I was browsing through the library's beautiful digital archive of drawings and art—which includes scans from many rare books—and an idea struck: Why not have artwork from this archive printed on fabric and then make myself a skirt to wear to the event? My next thought was something like: Why do these ideas always strike at the very last minute? I justified my frantic effort over the course of the next few days by reminding myself of the upside: It wouldn't take me long to get dressed for the event because my outfit was already planned.

I chose a beautiful century-old illustration showing the multi-leveled library and its delicate system of pulleys and tracks that carry books from floor to floor, and serious, buttoned-up, scholarly men studying books from the library's storied collections. I paid a small usage fee, downloaded a high-resolution version of the illustration, and then uploaded it to my Spoonflower account. After I chose the way I wanted the artwork to be repeated across the fabric, I ordered two yards on cotton sateen, which arrived just in time to be cut, sewn, and worn. As I made the skirt, I wondered what these serious, buttoned-up, scholarly men would think about my project. In their day, the stately New York Public Library housed and protected books and artwork that, in some cases, existed in only one place in the whole world. Could these men have even imagined how information and art would be collected and shared today? And what we would be able to do with it? It was tempting to make the skirt a modest ankle length in honor of their bygone era, but when I noticed that there weren't any women depicted in the illustration, I decided to shake things up and go short and poufy. Besides, I only had the two yards.

Thus began my love affair with digital printing. Shortly after the library experiment, I started to print my own designs on fabric—which was especially appealing since many of the designs had been discontinued long ago by the fabric companies that originally manufactured them. Then I began to look for digital printing opportunities beyond fabric and discovered ideas in lots of creative fields. I was delighted to find that I could upload artwork to a print-on-demand wallpaper company and receive high-quality one-of-a-kind wallpaper. I also became aware of advancements in printing at home on desktop inkjet printers, which opened up lots of great crafting opportunities. For instance, I have been printing my own holiday cards on my inkjet printer for years, but I started to ask myself, why not go beyond the holiday cards? Why not print wrapping paper? And gift tags? Why not decoupage with the printed paper? Or print on different types of paper, like rice paper or vellum? Project ideas began to stack up in my mind until there were more than enough to fill a book. And best of all, I came to realize that this type of book would be a perfect way for me to share some of my long out-of-print fabric designs and illustrations on a disc, which is something I've been wanting to do for years.

Since not all of us are uber tech-savvy, I've tried to make this book as easy to use as possible. In the first section you'll find step-by-step instructions for making the projects, all of which require the use of the files on the disc enclosed in the book. There are several design options for most projects—in order to see which options are available, turn to the index on pages 98 to 105. Once you've decided on your design, you simply pop the disc into your computer, download the design, and away you go.

For those of you who have dreamed of creating their very own designs, you will also find a section on how to do that using Photoshop (see page 76). The method shown here is the one that I use to create repeating designs, but it's certainly not the only one; you may want to learn other methods later. Whether you're looking to become a professional designer or want to create artwork for fun, my hope is that this method will get you started. With a little practice, you'll soon be uploading your very own designs and printing yards of fabric, or making the paper projects in this book with your very own prints.

What I really love about this book is that it bridges the gap between hand-craft and the digital era. *Heather Ross Prints* will sit comfortably alongside sewing, scrapbooking, and DIY titles, but it makes use of printers and computers just as much as it does sewing machines and decoupage glue. Who would have thought that it would be possible to happily merge the satisfying feeling of making something by hand with the convenience of a speedy Internet connection? Certainly not those buttoned-up, scholarly men, I'm guessing.

GETTING STARTED

Each project shown in this book is made using artwork on the enclosed disc. Once you've inserted the disc into your computer, it's easier than you think to start crafting! But before you dive into the projects, you'll want to read through this overview of the process and gather your tools and materials.

HOW TO USE THE DISC

The disc that comes with this book contains two folders: Folder A: Prints for Projects; and Folder B: Additional Heather Ross Prints. The files in Folder A are preformatted to work with each project in the book, and they are ready to open and use without any alterations on your part. They can be opened using the free Adobe Acrobat Reader program as well as most image editing programs. In many projects, I have included several artwork options that aren't shown in the photographs. To see all of the artwork options available for each project, check the index on pages 98 to 105.

How you print the artwork from Folder A will depend on the type of project you are making. For paper projects, such as the Stitched Journal on page 41 or the Wrapped Gifts on page 73, you will simply print the design on paper using a desktop inkjet printer. For projects that require fabric, such as the Fabric-Covered Bamboo Tray on page 21 or the Summer Crickets Nightgown on page 53, you will need to upload the art to an on-demand digital printing service, which can print on all sorts of fabrics. I used Spoonflower.com to digitally print all of the fabrics shown in this book, and I have set up a page on their website specifically for use with this book (www.spoonflower.com/profiles/heatherross). In order to print any of the fabrics shown here, simply go to the Spoonflower site and order as much (or as little!) of the fabric as you need for your project. (Note that the instructions for each project will tell you how much and what kind of fabric you need.) Spoonflower also allows you to customize art files on their site with simple-to-use editing tools, so you can change the direction of the artwork, reduce or enlarge the scale, and in many cases, change the way it repeats across your fabric. If you want to have fabric printed through a site other than Spoonflower, you can simply upload files from Folder A to the site—just make sure the artwork is set at 300 dpi.

I have also set up a page on DesignYourWall.com, where you can order wallpapers using my designs, like the wallpaper shown on page 23. You can choose from a few different types of sturdy, high-quality wallpapers, including the conventional variety that is applied with paste, as well as a "peel-and-stick" paper.

The other folder on the disc—Folder B—contains a huge selection of my designs. You can use these in any way you please, such as printing fabric yardage for sewing projects, or printing the designs on paper. In many cases, you can substitute the prints called for in the projects with these alternate prints, or use them for any other crafty projects you can imagine. And if the artwork files on the disc are not enough to satiate you, be sure to check out the Design section on page 76 to learn how to create your own artwork using Photoshop. Then you can use your designs to make the projects in the book (or anything else your heart desires).

TOOLS AND MATERIALS

To complete the projects in this book, you will need access to a computer and some basic craft materials and tools. You can find out exactly which supplies you will need in the materials list that accompanies each project, but the list that follows outlines the most common tools and materials used in this book, all of which make great additions to any crafting space or studio. For help finding any of these tools and materials, check the Sources for Supplies on page 110.

Computers and Software

To open any of the art files found on the disc, you will need a desktop computer (either PC or Mac) and Adobe Acrobat Reader (which can be downloaded for free at http://get.adobe.com/reader/). For projects that can be personalized (such as the Stationery Suite on page 27 or the Personalized Notepads on page 51), you will be able to edit the text in the PDF. It's helpful if your computer is no more than a few years old and has an operating system that has been updated in the past year. You can view system and memory requirements on the Adobe Acrobat Reader website; this program uses minimal amounts of both. Still, a system that is current will make for a smooth and enjoyable experience.

If you do not have a computer at home or at work, another option is to take a graphic design class at a local community college—that way you will not only have an introduction to the basics of graphic design, but you will also have access to a computer. And as a student, you may qualify for deeply discounted rates on software and equipment purchases.

Printers, Inks, and Papers

Many of the projects in the book require the use of a desktop inkjet printer. With current inkjet printing technology, it's possible to print extremely high-quality images, especially if you take the time to familiarize yourself with the printer settings. Most leading printer companies—such as Canon, Epson, and Hewlett-Packard—make a wide variety of affordable desktop inkjet printers, and also produce papers and inks designed for use with them. Most of the paper projects in this book are made using a printer with a standard 9" (23 cm)-width feed, though you may also want to invest in a wider format printer (13" [33 cm] will be more than enough!) if you are planning to make lots of large printed projects, like the Fabric-Bound Sketchbook on page 67 or the large Rice Paper Lantern on page 35. (If you don't have a wide-format printer, you can make do by overlapping several 8½" x 11" [A4] printouts, trimming off their white borders, and attaching them with glue or double-sided tape to create a larger sheet.) Some specialty papers—especially ones that are very fine, very thick, or slippery—are difficult to print on because the rollers can't grip the paper and move it from the stack up to the printing area. If you plan to print on specialty papers, it's best to use an inkjet printer with a manual feed slot, which will help move the paper into the printer area smoothly. The manual feed slot will also enable you to print on extra-long pieces of paper (you may need to specify the length in Acrobat's "Page Setup" window).

A printer usually only accepts the type of ink cartridge that was created specifically for it. I highly recommend using an inkjet printer that uses at least six ink cartridges. Typically, these cartridges will include cyan, magenta, yellow, and black, plus lighter versions of cyan and magenta. It will cost a bit more, but will yield much higher-quality color than what you'll get with just the four basic colors.

I have found that I get the best results by using papers specifically designed for my printers, which seem to be about the same price as the non-brand-specific papers. Many of the specialty papers available are designed to simulate the glossy sheen of printed photographs, but I avoid these when printing artwork, instead using "matte" and "fine art" papers. These papers give printouts amazing color and detail. For optimal results, I recommend setting your printer specifically to print on that type of paper—an option on some newer machines—or using the "photo paper/matte" setting.

Additionally, I have used textured and transparent papers, such as vellum and rice paper, for some of the projects in this book, such as the Decoupaged Children's Storage Stool on page 45 and the Votive Holders on page 63. Vellum papers are available in letter-size (or A4) sheets at specialty paper and art supply stores. Rice paper, however, comes in larger sheets or on rolls, which will often need to be cut down to size and fed into the printer manually.

Sewing Machines and Tools

The sewing projects in this book were all made using a very basic mechanical sewing machine. Regardless of brand or the year it was manufactured, your machine should be fine as long as it can sew a straight stitch and a zigzag stitch, and you can easily adjust the stitch length and width, and thread tension. And, of course, you'll need to know how to thread your machine and load a bobbin correctly. In my years of teaching sewing, I have found that when a machine isn't stitching properly, it's usually because it hasn't been threaded correctly. Every machine is a little different, so be sure to consult your manual and follow its threading diagram carefully.

You will also need:

• Pair of sharp scissors and/or a rotary cutter and cutting mat
• Universal-point sewing machine needle
• Seam ripper

BASIC SEWING TOOLS

1. Fabric Scissors
2. Pinking Shears
3. Seam Ripper
4. Straight Pins
5. Hand-Sewing Needles
6. Bobbins
7. Thread
8. Tape Measure
9. Tracing Wheel
10. Rotary Cutter
11. Bias Tape Maker

BASIC CRAFTING SUPPLIES

1. Straight-Edge Ruler
2. X-Acto Knife
3. Scissors
4. Washi Tape
5. Brushes
6. Decoupage Glue
7. Mechanical Pencil
8. Japanese Calligraphy Brush
9. Wooden Bone Folder
10. Photo Mount Spray Adhesive

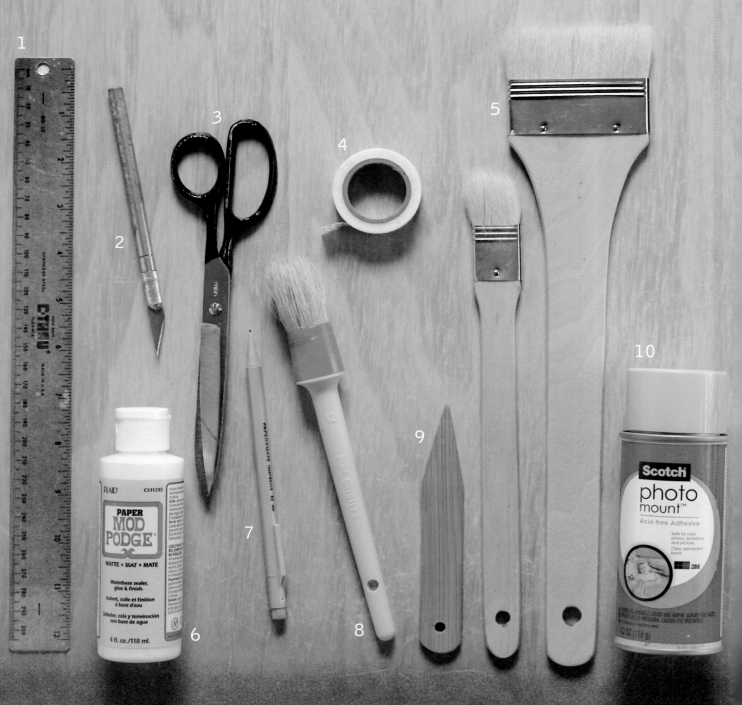

- All-purpose thread
- Straight pins
- Hand-sewing needles
- Disappearing-ink fabric pen
- Tape measure

Basic Craft Supplies

Here is a list of common supplies and tools, all of which can be acquired at your local craft shop.

CUTTING TOOLS

I use an assortment of tools to cut papers and fabrics. For cutting fabric, I use a pair of stainless-steel scissors (which can be sharpened). I keep several pairs of inexpensive plastic-handled scissors on hand for cutting paper. I also use inexpensive pinking shears—one pair for fabric, another for paper—for trimming raw edges on my seams (which keeps the fabric from unraveling) and for making decorative edges on paper. When the pinking shears become dull, I toss them away since they can't be sharpened. I use a rotary cutter on very slippery fabrics and when cutting several layers of fabric at a time. For paper projects that require precise cuts, I keep X-Acto knives and extra blades handy.

For making neat, consistent cuts through several sheets of paper at a time, I like to use a long-arm guillotine-style paper cutter. I recommend getting one that measures 18" (46 cm) square. Be sure that it has a locking mechanism on its arm, and that it is kept well out of reach of children. If you do not have a guillotine-style paper cutter at home, you can usually find one for public use at a FedEx Office store. Alternatively, you could use an X-Acto knife and straight edge, but the cut edges will not be as clean.

STRAIGHT-EDGE AND TRANSPARENT QUILTER'S RULER

I like to use both of these types of rulers for different reasons. The quilter's ruler is plastic and transparent, for times when I need to see exactly what I'm cutting through the ruler; this is great for use with a rotary cutter. The straight-edge ruler is made of steel, which is better to use with an X-Acto knife since the sharp blade can't become lodged in its edge.

LARGE CUTTING MAT

This is a craft room must. I use mine with rotary cutters, X-Acto knives, and box cutters, and as a hard surface when scoring paper or fabric.

BONE FOLDER

This is used for creasing paper. It's one of those tools that you might roll your eyes at, but once you actually try one and see how sharp the crease is, you'll realize that you can't live without it!

GLUES, ADHESIVES, AND TAPES

I keep several types of glue in my studio at all times, including basic staples like white glue and a glue stick. Decoupage glue dries perfectly clear over most surfaces (and some brands even come with a handy brush applicator!); Photo Mount spray adhesive, which comes in an aerosol can, is great for attaching photos to stiff surfaces.

Sometimes it makes more sense to use tape to hold papers together. In those cases, I tend to reach for double-sided tape, since you can hide the tape beneath the paper and still achieve a smooth surface. For more strength, I use double-coated tape, which has a much stickier surface. I also love using washi tape—a Japanese paper tape that is typically printed with a pretty design—though admittedly it's more for decoration than for strength.

PAINTBRUSHES

I buy paintbrushes and inexpensive foam brushes in a wide variety of sizes—from tiny to as big as a housepainting brush!—for applying glues and adhesives. I clean them immediately after use with warm water and dish soap and reuse them until they become crunchy and stiff.

She awoke in the woods with new friends to ...

PART ONE
PROJECTS

Finished Dimensions
Makes four 15" x 26" (38.1 cm x 66 cm) dishtowels

Materials
Panel of "Snow White Dishtowels" printed on linen-cotton canvas (see the index on page 98; note that one panel contains all four designs)

Scissors, or rotary cutter and cutting mat

Iron

Sewing machine

All-purpose thread (natural-colored thread blends best with most prints)

SNOW WHITE'S MONOGRAMMED DISHTOWELS

With seven dwarfs to look after, Snow White undoubtedly spent a great deal of time doing dishes, so it seemed appropriate to put Snow and her little charges on a stack of sturdy dishtowels. I'm a sucker for monograms, so I've included artwork with each and every letter of the alphabet so that nobody feels left out.

❶ Cut Out Dishtowels
The four dishtowels will come printed on one panel of fabric (see fig. 1). Using scissors or a rotary cutter and mat, carefully cut apart the four dishtowels.

❷ Hem Dishtowels
Turn the top edge of one towel ¼" (6 mm) to the wrong side and press, then turn again ½" (1.3 cm) and press. Edgestitch along this seam. Repeat with the other three edges of the dishtowel. Sew the other three dishtowels the same way.

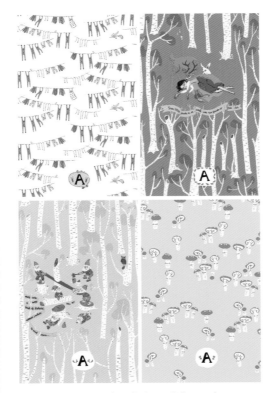

FIG 1 Fabric panel with four dishtowels.

Materials

9½" x 12½" (24.1 cm x 31.8 cm) bamboo tray (see Sources for Supplies, page 110)

Fat quarter of "Frog Meadow, Cream" printed on linen-cotton canvas (see the index on page 99; note that any design from Folder B on the disc can be used instead)

Pencil

Scissors

Newsprint or scrap paper

Foam brush, at least 1" (2.5 cm) wide

Decoupage glue

Fine-grit sandpaper (I like to use a sandpaper block or sanding sponge)

Rotary cutter and cutting mat

Spray lacquer, clear satin finish (I used Watco)

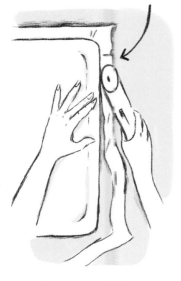

FIG 1 Trim excess fabric from tray.

FABRIC-COVERED BAMBOO TRAY

For this project, I covered a basic bamboo tray with a linen-cotton canvas floral fabric, and then sealed it with a spray lacquer so the tray can be wiped clean. I used a tray that is about 9½" x 12½" (24.1 cm x 31.8 cm), though you can use this technique on any size tray you like—just make sure you have enough fabric to cover its surface.

❶ Trace Tray Shape Onto Fabric

Make sure your tray is clean and dry. Lay the fabric face down on a work surface and place the tray face down on the fabric. Use a pencil to trace around the tray, adding an extra ¾" (2 cm) all the way around.

❷ Cut Out and Decoupage Fabric

Using scissors, cut out your fabric along the traced line, and place it right side down on a piece of newsprint or scrap paper. Use the foam brush to cover the wrong side of the fabric completely with a thin coat of decoupage glue, then quickly press the fabric onto the top side of the tray. Use your fingers to push the fabric into the curves of the tray as the glue sets.

❸ Trim Fabric and Sand Edges

Allow the tray to dry overnight. When the glue is completely dry, turn the tray over so that the fabric is face down. Place the tray on a cutting mat and use a rotary cutter to carefully trim the excess fabric off of the edge of the tray *(see fig. 1)*. Use fine-grit sandpaper to smooth the edges.

❹ Lacquer Tray

Set the tray fabric side up on newsprint or scrap paper, and spray a thin coat of lacquer onto the fabric. Allow the lacquer to dry and spray again. The fabric surface should be stiff to the touch when dry. The tray will be somewhat water-resistant, but should not be washed or submerged in water. You can use a damp cloth to clean the finished tray.

Materials

"Unicorns, Orange" printed on self-adhesive contact wallpaper (30" [76.2 cm] width) from www.designyourwall.com (see the index on page 99; note that the DYW website will provide information on calculating yardage)

Tape measure

Level (at least 48" [1.2 meters] long, with a "plumb sight" at its center)

Ladder or step stool (tall enough to allow you to reach your ceiling easily)

Pencil

Scissors

Washi tape

X-Acto knife with a very sharp blade

Wallpaper fell out of fashion for a few decades, partly because it was difficult to paste up and almost impossible to take down. But now wallpaper is making a comeback, and thanks to digital printing, you can put just about any design you want on your walls. Best of all, there is a new type of wallpaper on the market today: peel-and-stick! It's a sturdy vinyl contact paper with a peel-off backing, so you don't need any paste or water to make it adhere to your walls. And if you ever decide to take the paper down, you can remove it in just minutes with no tools or chemicals.

❶ Print Wallpaper

In order to create the unicorn wallpaper shown here, you can simply upload the pattern from the disc to a print-on-demand website (I like to use www.designyourwall.com). When you upload the file, the website will provide information for calculating yardage. Also, note that the directions presented here are for hanging paper on a single wall—a method I prefer when using a busy or bold print—but you can visit the DYW website for more information on how to paper a whole room.

❷ Locate Plumb Line

Working at eye level, measure 28" (71.1 cm) from the left corner of your wall, and make a small mark using a pencil. Place your level vertically on the wall, matching its right edge to this mark *(see fig. 1, page 24)*. Adjust the level until your "plumb sight" window shows a perfectly centered bubble. Using the right edge of your level as a guide, carefully draw a line, and then extend this line to the ceiling and floor. This is your "plumb line."

❸ Cut and Roll Sheets of Wallpaper

Your wallpaper will come on one large sheet with dotted "cut lines" so that you can cut out your panels for hanging. Cut your printed wallpaper sections out carefully along these dotted lines, then tightly roll up each section. Use washi tape to secure each roll until you are ready to use it.

❹ Hang Your First Sheet of Wallpaper

Remove the washi tape from one roll. Peel back about 6" (15 cm) of the protective backing from the top edge *(see fig. 2, page 24)*. Starting on the top left side of your wall, allow the top 2" (5 cm) of paper to rest lightly against the ceiling or molding (this is excess paper that will be trimmed off later—the excess here is required because most walls aren't perfectly even). Make sure that the right edge of your paper is lined up with the plumb line, then begin to pull the backing away from the paper *(see fig. 3, page 24)*. Lightly press the left edge of the paper into the corner as you work. Pause every so often to make sure that the paper is going on evenly and smoothly and stays aligned with the plumb line. Sweep your hands from side to side and downward to press out any air bubbles *(see fig. 4)*. When you reach the bottom of the wall, allow 2" (5 cm) extra to hang loosely. This will be trimmed off later.

⑤ Continue Hanging Wallpaper

Hold the top edge of your next roll of paper next to the top edge of the strip you just applied, and match the repeat carefully, leaving at least 2" (5 cm) of excess paper at the top edge. The papers should not overlap; they should meet perfectly at their edges. Apply the second roll the same way you did the first one, but don't press the paper onto the wall along the top edge until you are sure that the paper is unrolling evenly against the right edge of your first sheet. Once you are sure that your edges are matched up, you can start pressing the paper onto the wall. If your paper isn't lining up properly, carefully pull it off the wall and try again.

Continue hanging strips until you have reached the other side of the wall. If your last strip is wider than the space it needs to cover, press the wallpaper as far as you can into the corner and leave the excess paper.

⑥ Trim Wallpaper

Using an X-Acto knife with a very sharp blade, carefully trim away any excess paper from the left and right sides of the wall *(see fig. 5)*. Then carefully cut away the excess wallpaper from the top and bottom of the wall. To remove the excess paper, peel both sides of the section's top edge carefully away from the wall, pulling evenly and quickly and using a downward motion.

plumb line

28" (71.1 cm)

take measurement
at eye level

FIG 1 Use a level to find your plumb line, and extend line to ceiling and floor.

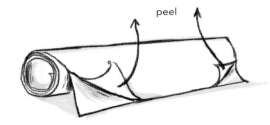

FIG 2 Peel backing away from first 6" (15 cm) of paper.

2" (5 cm)

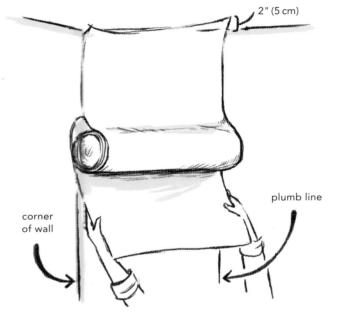

corner of wall

plumb line

FIG 3 Line up right edge of paper with plumb line.

FIG 4 Smooth paper against wall.

FIG 5 Trim away excess paper.

Materials

Inkjet printer

Pack of twenty-five 4½" x 6¼" (11.4 cm x 15.9 cm) notecards, in soft white

25 sheets of 8½" x 11" (or A4) matte presentation paper, for liners

3 packs of ten A6 envelopes

Guillotine-style paper cutter

Bone folder

Rounded-corner paper punch

Scrap paper

Glue stick

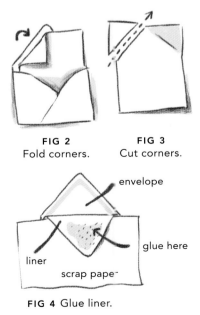

FIG 1 Slip printed liner into envelope.

FIG 2 Fold corners.

FIG 3 Cut corners.

FIG 4 Glue liner.

envelope

glue here

liner

scrap paper

STATIONERY SUITE

Customized notecards and matching envelopes are among my favorite gifts to give. Recently, I made a set to give to my niece, Mattie, who will be leaving home soon to go to college. I keep telling Mattie that once she is far away from her family she'll see how good it feels to get an actual piece of mail, but for now, Facebook is her preferred method of correspondence. Maybe these little bikes will change her mind.

① Print Notecards

Download the "Dream Bike" file from the disc and save it on your computer. If desired, you can personalize the notecard (for instance, adding a name or personal information).

Set your printer to "photo paper/matte," make your margins as small as possible, and print one copy on a notecard. Check to see that the artwork and text are centered, making adjustments if necessary in your page setup or printer settings windows, and print the remaining cards.

② Make Envelope Liners

Download the "Dots" file from the disc, and print out 25 copies on presentation paper. Cut the printed paper so that it measures 11" (27.9 cm) tall x 6¼" (15.9 cm) wide. Now open the envelope, and measure from the bottom edge to the tip of the flap, just below where the glue strip begins. Using a guillotine-style paper cutter, trim all 25 liner papers to this height.

Slip a printed liner paper into an envelope, with the right side facing out (*see fig. 1*). Fold down the top corners of the liner on both sides so that the folded edges run just below the glue line (*see fig. 2*). Use a bone folder to make sharp creases.

Remove the liner from the envelope, and cut off the corners along the creases (*see fig. 3*). Use the paper punch to create a rounded corner at the tip.

Insert the liner back into the envelope, and fold down the envelope flap (this will crease the liner at the fold). Lift up just the envelope flap, leaving the liner in place. Slide a piece of scrap paper under the liner (to protect the outside of the envelope from glue), and use a glue stick to apply glue to the edge of the liner (*see fig. 4*; note that it is only necessary to glue the liner's flap).

Close the envelope flap over the liner and press firmly to adhere the liner to the flap. Remove the scrap paper.

Repeat with each envelope and liner sheet.

Finished Dimensions

38" x 52" (96.5 cm x 132.1 cm), for duvet

20½" x 28" (52.1 cm x 71.1 cm), for pillowcase

Materials

1¼ yards (1.2 meters) of "Race Track" printed on 54" (140 cm)-wide linen/cotton blend fabric (see the index on page 100), for top of duvet cover

1¼ yards (1.2 meters) of solid, dotted, or striped 54" (140 cm)-wide fabric in a complimentary color, for duvet cover backing

1 yard (1 meter) of "Car Blobs" printed on 54" (140 cm)-wide linen/cotton blend fabric (see the index on page 100), for pillowcase

Rotary cutter and cutting mat, or scissors

All-purpose thread (natural-colored thread blends best with most prints)

Sewing machine

Iron

Disappearing-ink fabric pen

Four ⅜" (9 mm) plastic sew-on snaps

Hand-sewing needle

36" x 50" (91.4 cm x 127 cm) toddler duvet

Straight-edge ruler

Standard size pillow, 20" x 26" (50.8 cm x 66 cm)

TODDLER DUVET COVER AND PILLOWCASE

This pair of prints has always seemed to me like a perfect fabric combination for a little boy's bedding. It makes an especially great gift when paired with a few little toy cars like the ones that inspired these designs.

① Prewash Fabrics

Wash and dry duvet cover and pillowcase fabrics according to the manufacturer's instructions.

② Cut Fabrics for Duvet Cover

Using a rotary cutter and cutting mat (or scissors), trim off the selvedges from both pieces of the duvet cover fabric, and then cut both pieces so that they measure 54" (137 cm) long x 39" (99.1 cm) wide. (Note that if you use a different fabric design for this project, it will work best if the design does not have a strong vertical orientation since you're using the fabric's width for the duvet's length.)

③ Sew Duvet

With right sides facing, sew the duvet cover front and back fabric together along one long edge, across the bottom, and up the other long edge, using a ½" (1.3 cm) seam. Leave the top edge open.

④ Edgestitch Duvet Opening

Fold the top (open) edge of your duvet ½" (1.3 cm) to the wrong side to conceal the raw edges and press, then turn the edge another 1" (2.5 cm) and press. Edgestitch the edge of the top opening, sewing one continuous pass around the front and back panels. Turn the duvet right side out through the top opening.

⑤ Attach Snap Closures

Measuring from the top left corner of the duvet opening, use a disappearing-ink fabric pen to mark every 7½" (19.1 cm). Make your marks ½" (1.3 cm) from the top edge of the opening on both the front and back of the inside of the duvet cover. Use these marks to center your snaps, and hand-sew them to the duvet cover *(see fig. 1, page 30)*. Then stuff the duvet cover with the duvet, and close the snaps.

⑥ Cut Fabric for Pillowcase

Cut out your pillowcase fabric, creating one 43" x 34" (109.2 cm x 86.4 cm) piece of fabric.

⑦ Sew Pillowcase

Fold the fabric in half with the right sides facing, creating a 21½" x 34" (54.6 cm x 86.4 cm) rectangle. Using a ½" (1.3 cm) seam, sew along the top and left edges *(see fig. 2, page 30)*.

⊘ Edgestitch Pillowcase Opening

With the pillowcase still inside out, fold the open edge ½" (1.3 cm) to the wrong side and press, then turn back the edge another 5" (12.7 cm) and press. Edgestitch the opening, sewing one continuous pass around the front and back of the pillowcase *(see fig. 3)*. Turn the pillowcase right side out through the opening, and insert the pillow.

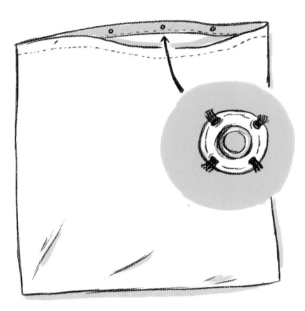

FIG 1 Hand-sew snaps to inside of duvet opening.

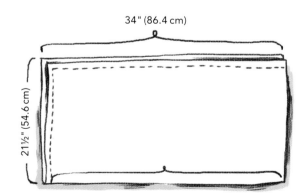

FIG 2 Sew top and left edges of pillowcase.

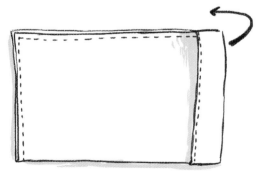

FIG 3 Edgestitch pillowcase opening.

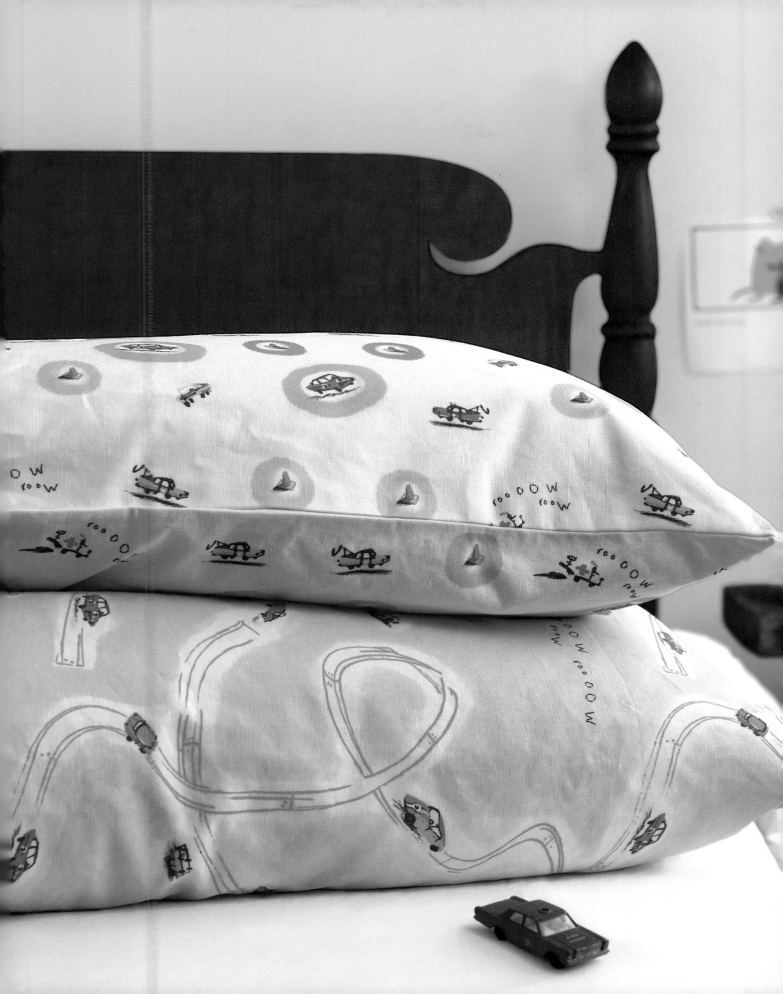

Finished Dimensions

Eight 12" (30.5 cm) square napkins (a great size for everyday use)

Materials

1 yard (1 meter) "Botanicals, Primary" printed on 54" (140 cm)-wide linen-cotton canvas (see the index on page 100; note that any design from Folder B on the disc can be used instead)

18" (45.7 cm) transparent ruler

Rotary cutter and cutting mat

Iron

Straight pins

White all-purpose thread

Sewing machine

Hand-sewing needle

2 yards (1.9 meters) each mini pom-pom trim in orange, yellow, green, and blue (see Sources for Supplies, page 110)

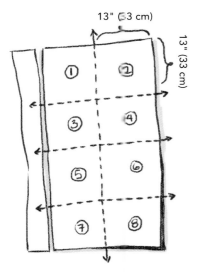

FIG 1 Cut fabric into eight squares.

LINEN-COTTON NAPKINS

I chose a floral print for these linen-cotton napkins, though you could use any print you like from Folder B on the enclosed disc (see the index on page 104). I added the tiny pom-pom fringe at the last minute—I found it at Purl Soho, and when I realized that the colors matched the print perfectly, I couldn't resist.

① Prewash Fabric

Wash, dry, and press the fabric according to the manufacturer's instructions.

Using a transparent ruler, rotary cutter, and cutting mat, measure the fabric and cut it into eight 13" (33 cm) square sections (see fig. 1).

② Press Napkin Edges

Turn and press all four sides of one napkin 1" (2.5 cm) to the wrong side to create fold lines, then open them up. Turn all of the corners down, so that their points meet the intersection of the pressed lines you just created, then trim ¼" (6 mm) from each corner (see fig. 2). Next, fold the top edge ¼" (6 mm) to the wrong side and press. Turn ¼" (6 mm) again and press. Repeat with the remaining edges, pinning in place as you go (see fig. 3).

Repeat with the seven remaining napkins.

③ Sew Napkin Edges

Starting at the top left corner of one napkin and using a medium-width stitch, edgestitch on the fold of the hem around your napkin. Repeat with the remaining napkins. Use a hand-sewing needle to close up each mitered corner.

④ Attach Pom-Pom Trim

Cut each piece of trim in half so that you have eight 1 yard (95 cm) lengths of trim.

Working on the napkin's wrong side, pin pom-pom trim in place along two edges of one napkin. Fold the raw edge of the trim under ⅛" (3 mm) at both ends, cutting the trim to fit. Use a medium-length zigzag stitch to sew trim into place.

Repeat to attach the trim to the remaining napkins.

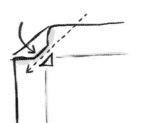

FIG 2 Fold corners to meet the crease lines and trim.

FIG 3 Fold edges ¼" (6 mm).

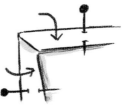

FIG 4 Fold edges another ¼" (6 mm).

Finished Dimensions

Small "Name in Lights" lanterns, 6" x 8" (15.2 cm x 20.3 cm)

Large lantern, 8" x 12" (20.3 cm x 30.5 cm)

Materials

For small "Name in Lights" lanterns:

1 string of white (not transparent) lights, with ½" (1.3 cm) bulbs spaced 12" (30.5 cm) apart (make sure that your string has enough bulbs for all of the letters you will be using)

6" (15.2 cm) lampshade bottom wire ring, and top ring with an uno-bridge style top (one for each lantern you will be making; see Sources for Supplies on page 110)

For large lantern:

One 3" (7.6 cm) white (not transparent) bulb or a 10' (3 meter) cord

One 8" (20.3 cm) lampshade bottom wire ring, and top ring with an uno-bridge style top (see Sources for Supplies on page 110)

For both lanterns:

Roll of rice paper or calligraphy paper

Inkjet printer

Scissors

Ruler

Pencil

Newsprint

Neutral pH adhesive

Small bowl

Paintbrush, ¼" (6 mm) diameter

RICE PAPER LANTERNS

I have always loved the way that printed rice paper lanterns softly filter light, so I was really excited when I figured out how to make them using my prints. For this project, I created two different types of lanterns: a larger size, which I like to hang as a single pendant light, and a smaller size, which works best when several are attached to "string lights." For the smaller lanterns, I created artwork with each letter of the alphabet, so you can literally spell out a person's name in lights.

❶ Print Design

Download the "Name in Lights" files from the disc for the smaller lanterns, or the "Lily, Plum" file for the large lantern (see index on page 100). For the smaller lanterns, you will need to download all of the letters that you need. Note that the large lantern files are specifically set up for wide-format printers or standard printers, so choose your files depending on the printer you have.

For the smaller lanterns, measure and mark one 7" x 25" (17.8 cm x 63.5 cm) sheet of rice paper or calligraphy paper for each lantern you will be making, then cut out the pieces with scissors. For the larger lantern, if you have a wide-format printer, measure and mark one 12½" x 37" (31.8 cm x 94 cm) piece of rice paper or calligraphy paper and cut it out with scissors. If you do not have a wide-format printer, measure and mark two 6½" x 37" (16.5 cm x 94 cm) pieces and cut them out with scissors. Print the 2 pieces separately, overlapping them by ½" (1.3 cm), and glue them together to get the required sheet size.

When printing the lanterns, make sure that your printer settings are set for "photo paper/matte" and that you are using the manual feed. Note that when you use the manual feed, you can print any length of paper, though you may need to specify the length that you are printing in your page setup window.

❷ Glue Lanterns

Wash and dry your hands thoroughly before starting. (You will be manipulating the paper while it is wet with glue, which will pull dirt off your skin and make it a permanent part of your craft project!)

Lay the printed rice paper right side down over a few pieces of newsprint. With the wrong side of the paper facing you, fold the top edge down ⅜" (9 mm). Repeat with the bottom edge (see fig. 1, page 36).

Pour a few spoonfuls of glue into a small bowl. Use the brush to spread glue into the crease of the bottom fold (see fig. 2, page 36). Carefully place the lampshade's bottom wire ring on top of the paper's bottom crease, and use your fingers to mold the paper up and over the ring (see fig. 3, page 36). (The paper will be very pliable from the moisture of the glue.) Continue folding the paper up over the ring until you have glued all the way around. Allow it to dry for 30 minutes, then repeat on the top edge with the top ring (*see fig. 4*). When you have glued all the way around the top ring, allow the edges of the paper to overlap about 1" (2.5 cm) and trim the remaining length of paper. Use the glue and brush to seal the opening (*see fig. 5*).

⚙ Insert Light
To attach the lanterns, unscrew each lightbulb from its socket and pull the socket through the uno top. Place the bulb inside the lantern, and screw it back into its socket (*see fig. 6*). Repeat with the remaining lanterns.

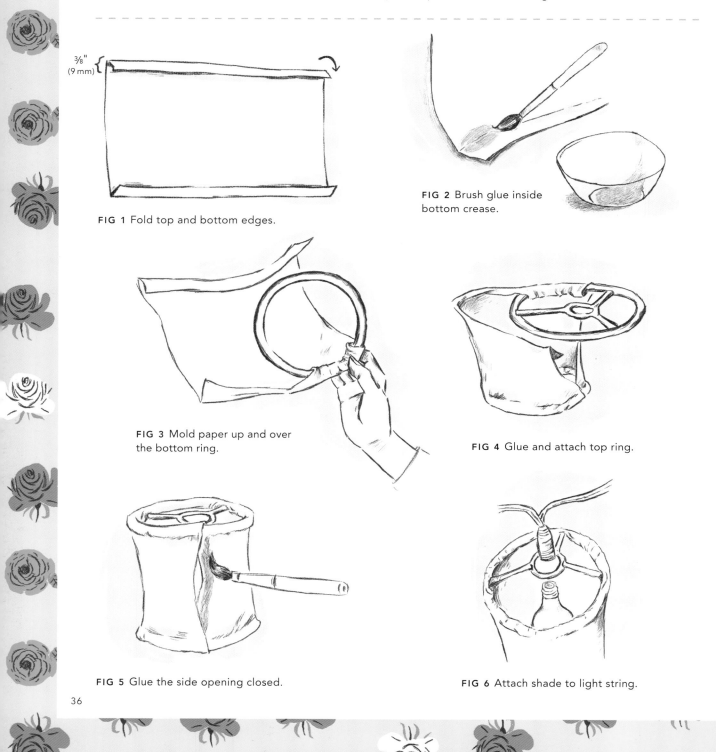

3/8"
(9 mm)

FIG 1 Fold top and bottom edges.

FIG 2 Brush glue inside bottom crease.

FIG 3 Mold paper up and over the bottom ring.

FIG 4 Glue and attach top ring.

FIG 5 Glue the side opening closed.

FIG 6 Attach shade to light string.

Finished Dimensions

68½" x 57" (1.74 meters x 1.45 meters)

Materials

2 yards (1.9 meters) "Underwater Sisters, Orange" printed on 58" (150 cm)-wide upholstery-weight cotton twill (see index on page 100; note that any design from Folder B on the disc can be used instead)

Rotary cutter and cutting mat

Iron

Sewing machine

Cotton-poly thread, to match

Pencil

Nine ⅜" (9 mm) grommets (plus a few extra in case they break) and a grommet tool (I like Dritz grommets and tools)

Shower curtain liner and 9 shower rings

UNDERWATER SISTERS SHOWER CURTAIN

For some reason, big bold prints always seem to work in a bathroom— not to mention that mermaids are truly at home swimming around a tub, no? This shower curtain is a great way to use extra-wide cotton twill from Spoonflower, since there is absolutely no waste and only very basic sewing skills are required. I added grommets to reinforce the holes along the top edge, but you can always keep things simple and use buttonholes instead.

① Prewash Fabric

Hand-wash the fabric in warm water (or machine-wash according to the manufacturer's instructions) and hang to dry. This will help to "true" the fibers of the fabric (see page 107). Once the fabric is dry, trim off any uneven edges at the top and bottom using a rotary cutter and cutting mat.

② Finish Edges

Turn the selvedge edges ½" (1.3 cm) to the wrong side, press, and edgestitch using a medium-length stitch.

Turn the bottom edge ½" (1.3 cm) to the wrong side and press. Turn another ½" (1.3 cm) to the wrong side and press, then edgestitch.

Turn the top edge ½" (1.3 cm) to the wrong side and press. Turn again 2" (5.1 cm), press, and edgestitch.

③ Add Grommets

Before you add the grommets, determine their placement along the top edge of the shower curtain. To do this, find the center of the panel, and use your pencil to mark a small "X" 1" (2.5 cm) from the top edge. Measure 1" (2.5 cm) from each side edge of the curtain top, and mark two more Xs, both 1" (2.5 cm) from the top edge of the curtain.

Now fold the first X to the center X, and mark the middle point between those two. Repeat on the opposite side (there are now 5 Xs total).

Fold each X to its neighboring X once more, and mark each of the middle points (there are now 9 Xs total).

Insert grommets at each of these marked points, following the manufacturer's instructions. Slip the shower rings through each grommet in the curtain and shower curtain liner, and hang.

VIOLET

icing to follow at

Hill Inn

semi-formal

She awoke in the woods with new friends to gu~~

FAR, FAR AWA

Finished Dimensions

Approximately 8" x 5½" (20.3 cm x 14 cm), after trimming

Materials

One 8½" x 11" (or A4) sheet Fine Art Paper

16 sheets of 8½" x 11" (or A4) paper, for interior pages (any type of paper can be used, as long as it's not too thick—you'll need to be able to puncture through a stack using an awl)

Bone folder

Binder clips

Ruler

Pencil

Awl (as sharp as possible) and cutting mat or cardboard

Waxed thread or heavy-duty sewing thread, in off-white

Bookbinding needle or embroidery needle

Guillotine-style paper cutter, or rotary cutter (with a new blade) and cutting mat

⅛" (3 mm)-diameter hole punch, with at least a ½" (1.3 cm) reach

1 yard (1 meter) of elastic cord

2" x 2" (5.1 cm x 5.1 cm) vellum envelope

Washi tape, for taping vellum envelope in place

Photo corners with adhesive backs

STITCHED JOURNAL

This simple handmade booklet is a perfect place to jot down all of your thoughts and sketches. It's hand-sewn and requires no special glues or adhesives to bind. I included several sheets of sketchbook paper for writing and drawing, and vellum for attaching photos. To attach the photos, I chose old-fashioned photo corners with adhesive backs (which stick nicely to vellum), and I taped a little envelope to the back cover of the journal for stashing the photo corners. An elastic cord keeps the journal cover closed securely.

① Print Papers

Download the "Snow White, Gray" file from the disc, and save it on your computer. Make sure your printer is set to "photo paper/matte," and print one copy on the 8½" x 11" (or A4) Fine Art Paper, using as narrow a border as possible.

② Fold Pages

Make a neat stack of the interior pages, and fold them in half so that they measure 8½" x 5½" (21 cm x 14 cm). Crease the folds using the bone folder. Then fold the cover so that the print is on the outside, and crease the fold *(see fig. 1, page 42)*.

③ Arrange Papers

Lay the cover on a work surface with the printed side facing down. Stack the interior papers on the cover, lining up the center folds as closely as possible. Secure the top and bottom of the center folds with binder clips.

④ Create Holes in Spine

Beginning ½" (1.3 cm) from the top edge, use a ruler and pencil to lightly mark every ¼" (6 mm) along your center fold *(see fig. 2, page 42)*.

Move the stack to a cutting mat or piece of cardboard, and use the awl to create holes at each ¼" (6 mm) mark. Puncture through all layers of paper, twisting the awl as you press it into the stack *(see fig. 3, page 42)*.

⑤ Sew the Spine

Cut a piece of waxed thread approximately 20" (50.8 cm) long. Thread the needle, and insert it into the first hole you created with the awl. Pull the needle through to the second hole, leaving a long thread tail, and secure the tail to the top of your booklet with the binder clip.

Sew in and out of the holes down to the bottom edge *(see fig. 4)*, sewing through every hole, then stitch back up to the top in the same way, filling in the skipped stitches. Tie the thread in a secure knot near the top hole on the inside of the journal, and trim the excess thread about ¼" (6 mm) from the knot.

6 Trim Edges
Close the book, and trim the edges using the guillotine-style paper cutter or rotary cutter and mat, cutting through all of the pages in the stack *(see fig. 5)*. Make sure to trim off the white border on the edges of the cover, but be careful not to cut through your stitching!

7 Add Elastic and Envelope
Use the hole punch to create two holes in the back cover, centered and ¼" (6 mm) from the top and bottom edges *(see fig. 6)*. Thread elastic through the holes and tie the ends in a knot on the inside of the cover. The cord should be relaxed, not stretched at all, but sitting snugly against the top and bottom edge of the cover.

On the inside of the back cover, use washi tape to secure a vellum envelope over the knot as shown opposite. Fill the envelope with photo corners.

bone folder

FIG 1 Crease center folds in paper.

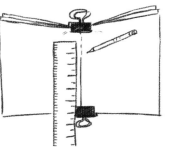

FIG 2 Mark every ¼" (6 mm) along center fold of interior papers.

cutting mat or cardboard

FIG 3 Create holes in spine with awl.

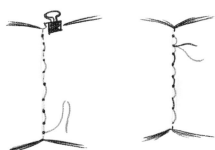

FIG 4 Sew spine.

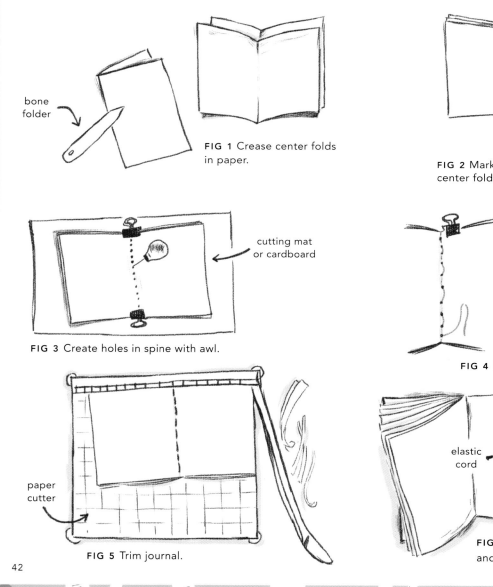

paper cutter

FIG 5 Trim journal.

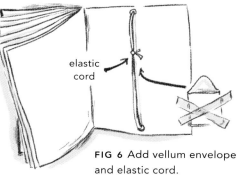

elastic cord

FIG 6 Add vellum envelope and elastic cord.

Materials

2 sheets 8½" x 11" (or A4) rice paper (vellum works well too, if rice paper is unavailable)

Inkjet printer

Scissors

Two-step storage stool (see Sources for Supplies, page 110)

Newsprint or scrap paper

Decoupage glue

Small bowl

Foam brush, at least 1" (2.5 cm) wide

Fine-grit sandpaper or sanding block

DECOUPAGED CHILDREN'S STORAGE STOOL

I have always loved the look of decoupaged kids' furniture, but I never had great results when I tried to make it until I learned this little trick: Use rice paper instead of regular paper. The reason it works so well is because rice paper is very porous and thin, becoming nearly translucent when the glue is applied. I chose to decoupage a storage stool, which is the perfect hiding space for little plastic horses (which clearly inspired the artwork I used for this project). The stool came in white, which matches the background of the artwork, making the print and the original stool color blend nicely. If you want to decoupage a darker stool with rice paper, keep in mind that the color of the stool may be visible behind the paper.

❶ Print Design
Download the "Playing Horses" artwork from the disc (see the index on page 101). Adjust your printer's settings to "photo paper/matte," and print the artwork onto two pieces of 8½" x 11" (or A4) rice paper or vellum.

❷ Cut Out Artwork
Using scissors, carefully cut out the "Playing Horses" artwork, leaving about ½" (1.3 cm) of space around the edge of each piece.

❸ Decoupage Stool
Set the stool on newsprint or scrap paper. Pour a small amount of decoupage glue into a small bowl, and use the foam brush to carefully apply glue to the back of one of the pieces of rice paper. Place the piece of rice paper on your stool, and smooth it in place with your fingertips. Continue to attach other pieces of rice paper in the same way until you are happy with the design. Allow the stool to dry, then brush a thin coat of decoupage glue over the entire surface of each piece of rice paper. Allow to dry, and repeat once more. Allow the stool to dry overnight.

Sand the edges of the decoupaged sections very carefully to smooth the dried glue, but be careful not to sand through the paper.

Materials

1 yard (91.4 cm) of "Repeating Roses, Pink" printed on 54" (140 cm)-wide linen-cotton canvas (see the index on page 101; note that any design from Folder B on the disc can be used instead)

Rotary cutter and cutting mat, or scissors

Sewing machine with buttonhole foot

All-purpose thread, to match background color

Iron

Disappearing-ink fabric pen

Two ¾" (1.9 cm)-diameter buttons

Sewing needle and thread

Straight pins

PINK ROSE APRON

This apron is based on one I was given to wear while helping with dinner at a friend's house. I loved its simple shape and that there was no center panel sliding around, unable to decide which side of my chest to cover. (That's always been my biggest gripe with aprons.) This apron is made from a simple rectangle of fabric, so there are no pattern pieces to trace and cut out and no fabric is wasted. And if you ever get tired of wearing it, you can cut off the straps and use it as a picnic blanket!

❶ Prewash Fabric and Make Straps

Wash and dry the fabric according to the manufacturer's instructions.

Lay out your 36" (91.4 cm)-wide x 54" (140 cm)-long panel. Using a rotary cutter and cutting mat or scissors, trim the fabric to a 34" x 46" (86.4 cm x 116.9 cm) rectangle, trimming off the selvedges. Cut a 3" (7.6 cm) strip from the short edge of the fabric (*see fig. 1*). Fold the strip in half lengthwise, with right sides together. Stitch the long edges together with a ⅜" (9 mm) seam. Turn the strip right side out, and press. Cut the strip in half to create two 17" (43.2 cm) straps. Set the straps aside.

❷ Finish Edges

Turn one edge of the fabric ¼" (6 mm) to the wrong side and press, then turn again ½" (1.27 cm) and press. Edgestitch using a medium-length stitch. Finish the other three edges in the same way.

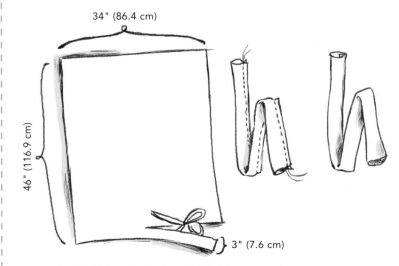

FIG 1 Cut 3" (7.6 cm) strip from fabric's bottom edge; fold the strip, sew, and turn right side out.

3 Make Buttonholes

Lay out the fabric right side down so it is 32½" (82.6 cm) tall and 41½" (105.4 cm) wide, and fold the sides to meet. Attach the buttonhole foot to your sewing machine. Make two side-by-side ¾" (1.9 cm)-wide buttonholes (see Making Buttonholes, page 108) on the top left corner where the edges meet *(see fig. 2)*; both buttonholes should be 1¼" (3.2 cm) from the top edge, and 2" (5.1 cm) and 4" (10.2 cm) from the side edge, respectively.

4 Attach Buttons

The trick to a flattering fit is the placement of the buttons on the back. Have a friend help you wrap the panel around your chest so that the two edges overlap in the back. Pin the apron in place, and mark the spots where the buttons will go with a disappearing-ink fabric pen. The button closest to the edge should be placed slightly higher than the other to create a subtle "A-line" shape. Sew on the buttons (see Sewing on Buttons, page 109).

5 Attach Straps

Once the buttons are attached, put the apron on, turn the ends of the straps under, and pin the straps to the inside front of the apron. With your friend's help, pin them in place on the back. Machine-sew the straps into place, stitching a rectangle *(see fig. 3)*, or attach the straps using a sewing needle and thread.

FIG 2 Make buttonholes and attach buttons.

32½" (82.6 cm)

41½" (105.4 cm)

FIG 3 Stitch rectangle to attach straps.

vera mclaughlin

FOR VER

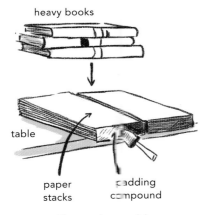

heavy books

table

paper
stacks

padding
compound

FIG 1 Notepad assembly.

PERSONALIZED NOTEPADS

Padding compound is one of my favorite new discoveries. It's an adhesive used to bind together papers and create a "pad," and it can be found in the bookbinding section of most craft stores (or you can order it online; see the Sources for Supplies on page 110). In no time, you'll have your very own adorable personalized pad on which to scribble notes.

① Print Papers

Download the "Underwater Sisters" file from the disc and save it on your computer. If desired, you can personalize the notepad (for instance, adding a name or personal information).

Set your printer to "plain paper" and print 1 page to test the file. Cut the paper in half into two 8½" x 5½" (or 21 cm x 14.9 cm) pieces to make sure that the margins are lining up correctly. If the images and text on both pages look good, print the remaining 79 pages. If the image does not look right, or if the image is printing too close to the paper's edge, open up your "print" window again and review your preview image. You should be printing the image at its full size with no scaling, and you should have the "landscape" option turned on.

② Cut Papers

Using a paper cutter, cut the remaining 79 pages in half into 8½" x 5½" (or 21 cm x 14.9 cm) pieces. Cut the papers in stacks of 5 to 10 pages at a time (depending on your cutter's ability to keep them evenly stacked as they are cut). Make two stacks of cut pages, one with each design.

③ Assemble Notepads

Using the paper cutter, cut the chipboard in half into two 8½" x 5½" (or 21 cm x 14.9 cm) pieces. Place each stack of printed pages on top of each piece of chipboard. Pick up each stack and "tap" its top edge against a flat surface so that the pages and chipboard line up evenly, then place them on the table so that the top edge sits just slightly past the table's edge. Now place your stack of heavy books on top of your "pads."

④ Glue Pads

Put a few spoonfuls of padding compound into a small bowl, and coat the foam brush with it. Using light strokes, brush the padding compound onto the edge of your pads *(see fig. 1)*. Don't worry about the compound going past the edge and onto the first sheet of paper or the chipboard backside—it will become invisible when it dries. Allow the compound to sit for at least 1 hour before touching it. Once the pad is dry, you're ready to use it.

Finished Dimensions

Small/Medium: Fits bust up to 36" (91.4 cm), hip up to 41" (104.1 cm)

Medium/Large: Fits bust up to 38" (96.5 cm), hip up to 43" (109.2 cm)

Materials

"Nightgown Front" and "Nightgown Back" pattern pieces (available on the enclosed disc)

Transparent tape

Paper-cutting scissors

Disappearing-ink fabric pen

Rotary cutter and cutting mat

2 yards (1.9 meters) "Crickets" printed on 54" (140 cm)-wide silk crepe de Chine fabric (see the index on page 101; note that any design from Folder 3 on the disc can be used instead)

All-purpose thread, in white

Sewing machine with a sharp needle

3 yards (2.8 meters) fold-over elastic in coral

Straight pins

Iron

Hand-sewing needle

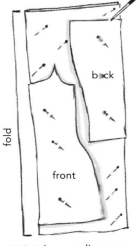

FIG 1 Layout diagram.

SUMMER CRICKETS NIGHTGOWN

I love falling asleep to the sound of cicadas and crickets coming through a screen window, so this print seemed natural for summer sleepwear. It's printed on a silk crepe de Chine fabric, which is as supple as it is strong, and insulates and breathes much better than cotton. It's a little slippery to work with, and for that reason I always use a fresh rotary cutter blade and an extra-sharp needle when starting a silk project. I used fold-over elastic to finish the edges and to make my straps, which I find much easier to work with—and much more comfortable to sleep in—than woven bias tape.

❶ Cut Out Pattern Pieces

Print out "Nightgown Front" and "Nightgown Back" pattern pieces from the disc (the pattern will print on several 8½" x 11" [21.6 cm x 27.9 cm] sheets of paper). Align the pattern pieces, and tape them together, then cut out your pattern pieces in your desired size.

Lay the pattern pieces on top of the fabric as shown in the layout diagram (*see fig. 1*), and trace the pattern pieces with a disappearing-ink fabric pen. Make sure to also transfer the bust dart lines onto the fabric. Use a rotary cutter and cutting mat to cut out your pieces along the traced lines.

❷ Sew Bust Darts

With right sides facing, press the bust dart, and stitch from the raw edges toward the endpoint of the dart (do not back-tack). Tie the thread tails in a double knot to secure both ends. Press the darts toward the hemline, and press the nightgown front flat (*see fig. 2, page 54*).

❸ Sew Nightgown

With right sides together, and using a ½" (1.3 cm) seam, sew the back pieces together along the center seam. Then, with right sides together, sew the front and back pieces together with a ½" (1.3 cm) seam, along the side seams.

To finish the bottom hem, turn and press the edge ¼" (6 mm) to the wrong side, then turn it again ¼" (6 mm), and edgestitch using a medium-length stitch.

❹ Add Elastic to Front

Cut a piece of fold-over elastic the length of the top front edge of the nightgown. Fold the elastic over the raw edge, and pin it into place (*see fig. 3, page 54*). Use a zigzag stitch to sew it onto the nightgown.

⑤ Add Elastic to Back and Make Straps

Leave 15" (38.1 cm) of the remaining elastic free, and starting from one top front edge, pin the elastic along the arm-hole edge, around the back edge, and along the other armhole edge, leaving another 15" (38.1 cm) length of elastic free at the opposite top front edge (see fig. 4). Then zigzag-stitch the elastic in place.

⑥ Finish Straps

Put the nightgown on, and have a friend pin the straps in place on the back, attaching them to the nightgown about 1" (2.5 cm) outside your shoulder blades (see fig. 5). Carefully remove nightgown, and hand-stitch the straps into place using a hand-sewing needle and thread.

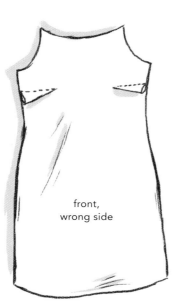

FIG 2 Sew bust darts.

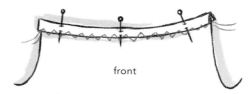

FIG 3 Attach fold-over elastic to top front edge.

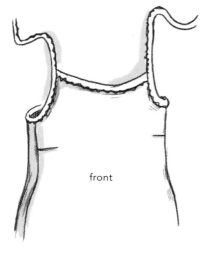

FIG 4 Attach elastic to arm-holes and back.

FIG 5 Finish straps.

Materials (to make a set of 9 interlocking cards)

1 sheet of 8½" x 11" (or A4) card stock

Inkjet printer

Sharp paper scissors

Heavy-duty box cutter with sharp blade and cutting mat

Straight-edge metal ruler

18 sheets of 8½" x 11" (or A4) Fine Art Paper

Nine 4½" x 6½" (11.4 cm x 16.5 cm) photos

9 pieces of 8" x 10" (20.3 cm x 25.4 cm) archival mounting board, 1/16" (2 mm) thick

Photo Mount spray adhesive

Heavy-duty guillotine-style paper cutter, at least 12" (30.5 cm) square

Pencil

Fine-grit sandpaper (I like to use a sanding block or sanding sponge)

(MY) HOUSE OF CARDS

This project was inspired by the famous "House of Cards" by Charles and Ray Eames—notched cards printed with iconic images from the fifties and sixties that linked together to create a house. For my set of cards, I kept the same concept, but printed cards with favorite personal photos and designs. Many of the childhood photos are scanned photographs that I blew up and printed, while the more recent image was taken with a digital camera and up-loaded directly to my computer.

① Print Card Template, Photos, and Designs

To create a cardstock template, download the template from the disc (see index on page 102), and print it on a piece of card stock. Using a box cutter with a straight-edge ruler on a cutting mat, cut out the template, then carefully cut out the curves and notches with sharp scissors.

Download the 9 files in the "My House of Cards" folder on the disc (see index on page 102), set your printer to "photo paper/matte," and print them on Fine Art Paper. Using a paper cutter, trim off the unprinted borders.

Scan 4½" x 6½" (11.4 cm x 16.5 cm) photos to your computer, or gather new digital photos (9 total). If desired, use imaging software (such as iPhoto or Picasa) to crop and scale your photos, "desaturate" (convert a color image to black and white), or make changes using filters that will add graininess, smoothness, or a variety of other textures and effects; print them on Fine Art Paper. Trim the photo printouts to 4½" x 6½" (11.4 cm x 16.5 cm).

② Attach Photos and Prints to Mounting Board

In a well-ventilated area, use spray adhesive to adhere one pattern print to a piece of mounting board, aligning one corner as perfectly as possible *(see fig. 1, page 58)*. On the other side of the mounting board, use spray adhesive to adhere one of your photos, using the same corner to align the edges. Smooth and press the paper onto the board to secure it.

Repeat with all the photos and prints on the remaining 8 mounting boards, and allow them to dry for at least 1 hour.

❷ Cut Out Cards

Trim 1 card to 4½" x 6½" (11.4 cm x 16.5 cm), using the photo as a cutting guide (for best results, use a guillotine-style paper cutter; if that is not available, use a box cutter and straight edge). Lay your template over the trimmed card, and use a sharp pencil to trace around the template onto the card (*see fig. 2*). The card and template should be roughly the same size, but you can use a box cutter and straight edge on a cutting mat to trim the long edges if they don't match exactly. Then use the paper scissors to cut out the rounded corners and notches. Use fine-grit sandpaper to carefully smooth the edges and corners. Repeat with the remaining cards.

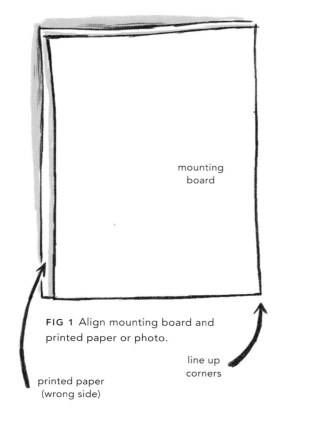

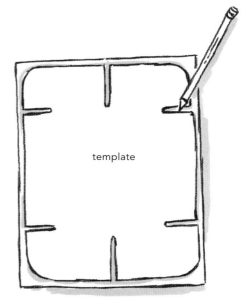

FIG 1 Align mounting board and printed paper or photo.

mounting board

printed paper (wrong side)

line up corners

FIG 2 Mark and cut notches.

template

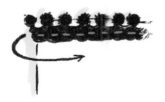

Finished Dimensions
52" (1.3 meters) wide x 49"
(1.2 meters) long

Materials

1½ yards (1.4 meters) "Water Ski
Beauties, Blue" printed on 54"
(140 cm)-wide cotton voile
(see the index on page 102;
note that any design from
Folder B on the disc can be
used instead)

Scissors or rotary cutter and
cutting mat

Sewing machine

Iron

All-purpose thread (natural-
colored thread blends best with
most prints)

Straight pins

1¾ yards (1.6 meters) pom-pom
trim in yellow

FIG 1 Tuck ends of pom-pom
trim under folded fabric.

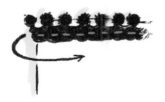

FIG 2 Sew trim to top edge.

WATER-SKI BEAUTIES VOILE SARONG

Lightweight sarongs are a great summer staple. I wear them as skirts, dresses, cover-ups, and even wrapped around my head. This project uses 2 yards (1.9 meters) of lovely cotton voile, which is airy and lightweight and dries very quickly in the sun, making it perfect for a day on the water. I chose the Water Ski Beauties print in a dark blue colorway and finished the top edge with a fun little pom-pom trim in bright yellow, which adds a nice detail when worn tied across the chest.

① Prewash and Cut Fabric
Wash and dry the fabric according to the manufacturer's instructions. Using your scissors or rotary cutter and cutting mat, trim off the selvedge edges, and trim the length of the fabric so it measures 51" (129.5 cm).

② Press Edges
Turn the sarong's side edges ½" (1.3 cm) to the wrong side, and press. Turn the fabric another ½" (1.3 cm) to the wrong side, and pin. Turn, press, and pin the top and bottom edges in the same way.

③ Add Pom-Pom Trim and Finish Edges
Tuck the ends of the pom-pom trim under the folded sides of the top edge of the fabric (*see fig. 1*), and pin the trim to the wrong side along the top edge. Beginning with the top right corner, stitch the pom-pom trim in place (*see fig. 2*), and then continue sewing along the folded edge around the other three sides.

Secure the pom-pom trim in place by stitching a second, parallel row just above the first row, as close to the top edge as possible.

① SCAN YOUR ARTWORK

Once you have your sketch worked out, you're ready to scan it and create your digital file. I recommend scanning at 360 dpi (dots per inch) in black and white. Once the artwork is scanned, open it up as a new file in Photoshop, set it as RGB, and save it.

② SET RESOLUTION AND PREFERENCES

From the menu bar at the top of the screen, click Image > Image Size, which will open up the Image Size dialogue box. Set the resolution and other preferences as shown in the screenshot *(see fig. 1)*.

③ ERASE UNNECESSARY LINES FROM ARTWORK

Click on the Eraser tool in the toolbar, and erase all of the lines that you don't plan to trace.

④ SCALE ARTWORK

Next, you'll need to scale your artwork, if necessary, so that it will be the same size that you want your finished artwork to be. If you're not sure, err on the larger side since you can scale

down later without losing resolution but your file will distort if you scale up later. To change the size of your sketch, use the Lasso or Marquee tool (in the toolbar) to select the artwork, then pull down the "Edit" menu from the menu bar, and select Transform > Scale. This will make little "handles" appear on all sides of your selected artwork. You can click on any one of these handles and move them in any direction to change the shape of your sketch *(see fig. 2)*. If you hold down the "Shift" key while simultaneously "pulling" on the handles, you will keep the original dimensions of your sketch intact. When the art is the size you want it to be, double-click on the selected area.

⑤ FAMILIARIZE YOURSELF WITH THE NAVIGATOR WINDOW

Now, use the Magnifying Glass tool from your toolbar to zoom in a little bit and get a closer look at your artwork. The window in the lower right corner with the red outline, which is called the Navigator, shows you where you are. You can use your cursor to move the red square around inside the Navigator window to change which part of your artwork is visible and to zoom in and out.

FIG 2 Pull on handles to scale artwork.

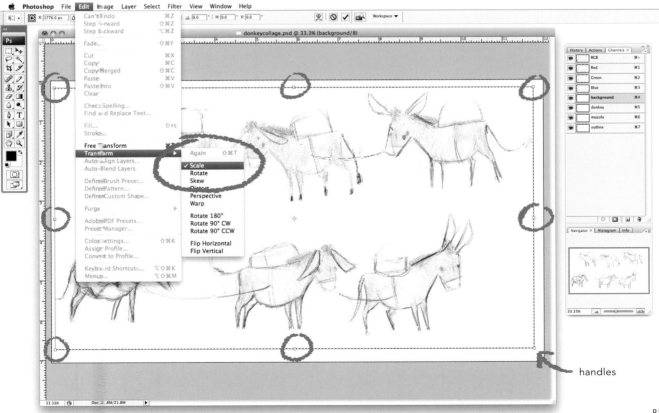

handles

⑥ SET THE IMAGE INTERPOLATION PREFERENCES

Setting the image interpolation preferences will allow you to move and scale your Photoshop artwork without creating annoying fuzzy edges. From the menu bar at the top of the screen, click: Photoshop > Preferences > Image Interpolation > Nearest Neighbor (preserve hard edges) *(see fig. 3)*.

⑦ START BUILDING SPOT CHANNELS

Now you're ready to start building your spot channels. A spot channel is basically a fancy name for "color"—each spot channel will be a single layer of color applied on top of your sketch. The spot channel method is very useful because it allows you to build artwork with clear, solid colors that can be easily adjusted and changed. Note that four spot channels (RGB, green, blue, and red) will already exist—these channels represent your original sketch.

To create a new spot channel, click on the small icon in the top right corner of the Channels window (the three horizontal lines right on top of each other), which will open the drop-down menu bar; select "New Spot Channel" *(see fig. 4)*.

Click on the small square of color inside the "New Spot Channel" box to open the "picker," and use your slider to choose a color. I usually start by selecting a dark brown or black color, which I will use as my "outline" color, though you can pick any color you want for outlining and shading. Set your solidity at

50%, which will allow you to see your sketch underneath your colors as you work *(see fig. 5)*. If you set your solidity at 100%, you won't be able to see anything hidden underneath another channel.

Make a few more spot channels before you begin working on your design. You can set your colors without much concern at this stage since you'll be going back and fine-tuning them later. For my donkey illustration, I'm going to try a lavender and gray color theme, so I'm making a lavender spot channel called "background" and a gray spot channel called "donkey." I'm also pretty convinced that I'm going to want my donkey to have a white-ish nose and belly, so I'm making a creamy white spot channel called "muzzle." I can add more channels later, but this will be enough to get me started.

Channels represent layers of colors, and the order in which they appear in your list determines the order of the layers. For instance, the channel at the top of the list will lie underneath all other colors, and the channel at the bottom will be visible over all your other colors. By moving the "outline" channel to the bottom of the list you can make sure that your lines will always show over your colors. I prefer to keep my "background" channel at the top of my list, so it stays underneath all of my other colors. You can move your channels by clicking just to the left of a channel's name (but inside the box that holds its name) and "dragging it" up or down *(see fig. 6; page 88)*.

FIG 3 Set image interpolation preferences.

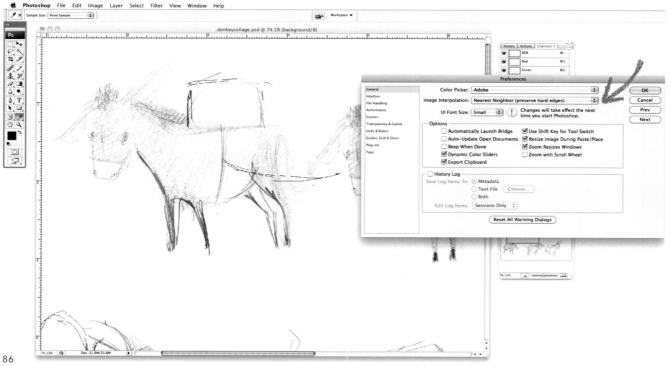

FIG 4 Build spot channels.

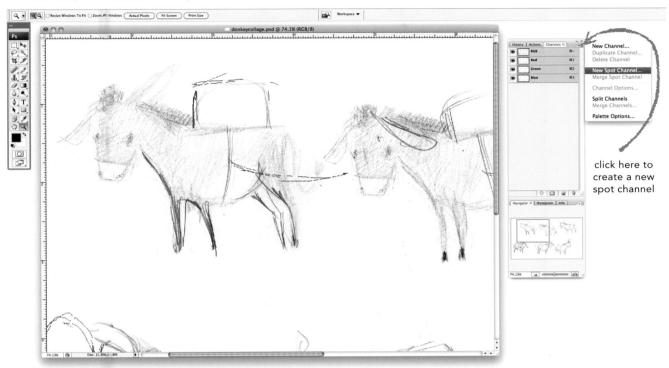

FIG 5 Pick colors and set solidity.

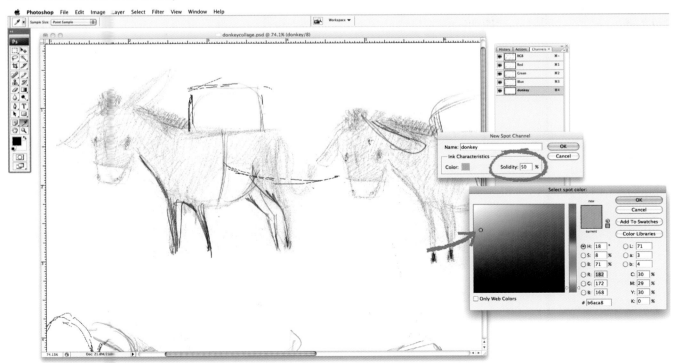

OUTLINE ILLUSTRATION AND FILL IN COLOR

There are several ways to fill an area with color in Photoshop. You can use your Pencil or Brush tool to "draw" and "paint" in color, or you can select an area using your Lasso or Marquee tool and click "Edit > Fill" from the menu bar to fill the area with color. Since I tend to use Photoshop to achieve a hand-drawn look, I prefer to use my Pencil tool to fill areas with color.

To set the size of your pencil tip, use the drop-down menu just under the main menu bar that appears next to the word *Brush*, as shown (*see fig. 7*). You must have the Pencil tool selected for this menu to appear! Experiment with different brush-tip sizes until you find one that works best, depending on whether you are filling in or outlining. In the case of the donkey artwork, I used a size-12 tip to fill in the donkey and to color in the background around him, and then I switched to a much bigger tip, a 38, to fill in the larger sections of background.

When you are ready to start adding color, you must first select a channel (or color). If you are drawing with a channel selected and aren't seeing any color appear, or if the color looks faded, check to make sure that the "picker" in the bottom of the toolbar is showing a pure black box in the foreground and a pure white box in the background. Any variation will change the opacity of your fill (*see fig. 7*). If you're still having problems drawing with channels, review the troubleshooting suggestions on the following page.

FIG 6 Adjust order of channels.

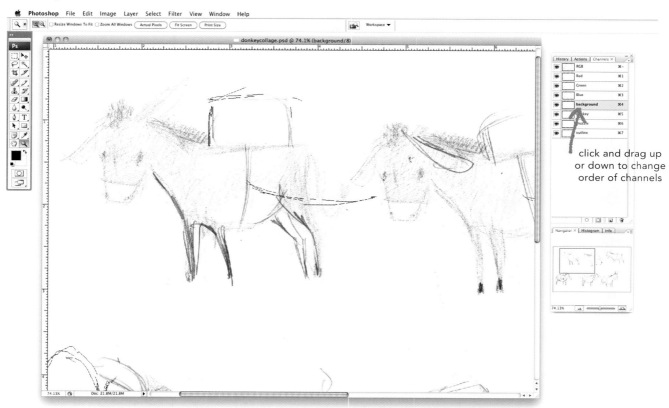

FIG 7 Pick channel and adjust brush-tip size.

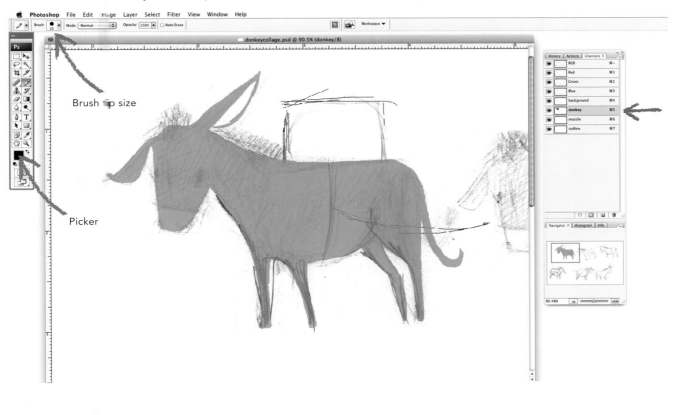

Troubleshooting in Channels

I'm using my Pencil tool to try to draw, but nothing appears when I do. What's wrong?

Look at the very bottom of your toolbar. See those two little boxes? When working in channels, the one in front should be black, and the one in back should be white. To reset them, click on the much smaller set of boxes, just to their lower left.

If that doesn't do the trick, check to make sure that you haven't left an active "selection" somewhere on your image. It's a common mistake to accidentally select such a tiny part of your artwork that the "blinking" lasso isn't even visible. You can make sure no selections are hiding by choosing Deselect (All) from the "Select" menu.

I'm trying to draw using my pencil, but the lines appear very faded and don't match the color that I set for this channel.

Check that the two little boxes at the bottom of your toolbar are set correctly; the box in front should be black, the one in

back should be white. If the color in front is any color other than black, then the lines you draw with your pencil are going to appear faded. This can happen sometimes if you click on the "black" box (which sets the color for "foreground") and select any of the colors in the picker; you'll know you've done this if the foreground box shows up as a gray tone. To reset the boxes, click on the much smaller set of boxes, just to the lower left.

My stylus doesn't seem to be working properly—sometimes it selects things when I want it to draw.

Most styluses have a clicker on them, like a mouse, that is easy to accidentally press. Read the instructions for your stylus to either learn the clicker features or to turn them off.

9 CLEAN UP EDGES

In the channels box, you can click on the little "eyeball" icons next to the first four channels (RGB, Red, Green, and Blue) to make your underlying sketch invisible; then clean up the edges of your color fill using the Pencil and Eraser tools *(see fig. 8)*. When you are done, click on the eyeball boxes again to make your sketch reappear. You can do this with any of the channels at any time.

10 ADD DETAILS

Once you've done some basic coloring-in over your sketch, you're ready to start adding details. Using the Pencil tool with a fine tip (I prefer size 5), select the "outline" channel and start adding details *(see fig. 9)*. If your drawing has a face, you may want to add eyes and a nose. I have found that no matter how proficient one becomes with a stylus, it's still very difficult (if not downright impossible) to draw a perfectly steady, even line in Photoshop, so it's important to embrace a more "hand-

drawn" style. I use short, sketchy lines to add detail, changing the size of my pencil when needed. You can zoom in very close to add details that are especially small or need extra attention, but as a rule, I avoid trying to make everything look even.

11 PLAY WITH COLORS

At this point, you can also start adding a few new channels and playing with colors. In my donkey illustration, I wanted to add some new colors to my baskets and experiment with changing my background color *(see fig. 10)*. Before trying out a new background color, save your file, and then save your file again under a different name (such as "donkeysorange.psd"). To change your background color, double-click on your "background" channel to open a selection window. If you click on the little square of color, it will take you back to the "picker" window, where you can use the slider tool to try other hues and then move your cursor around in the big color square to fine-tune your selection *(see fig. 11, page 92)*.

FIG 8 Make underlying sketch invisible.

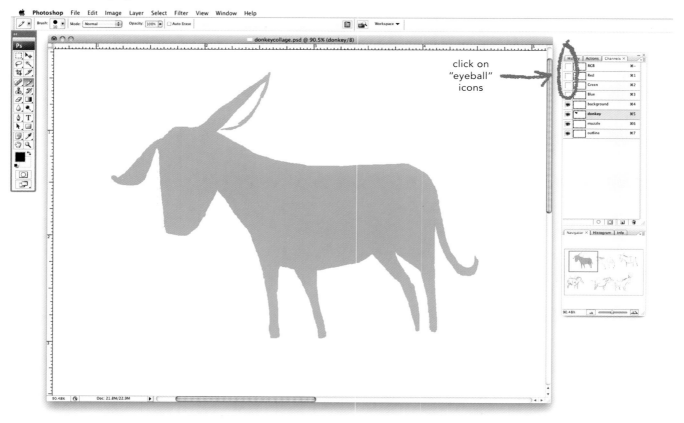

FIG 9 Use outline channel to add details.

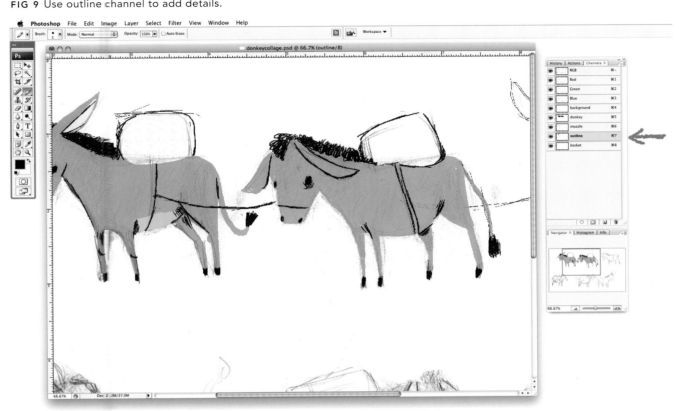

FIG 10 Experiment with background colors.

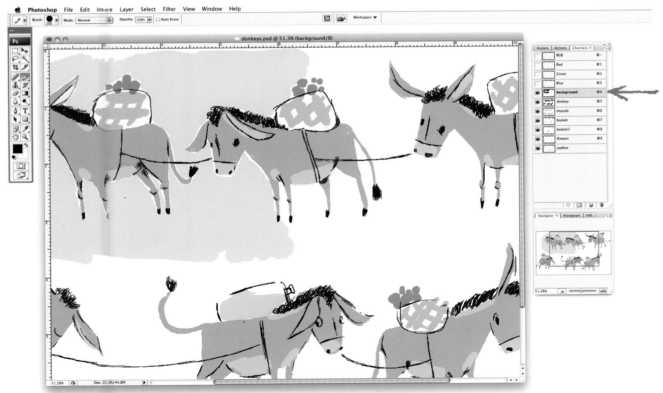

Remember that at any point, you can make your RGB channels (your original sketch) invisible to get a sense of how your finished artwork will look. Once you've created an option that you like, you'll want to save your file and turn your drawing into a design that can be repeated. And remember, you can go back and create endless color combinations later.

⑫ FINE-TUNE THE DESIGN

I'm noticing that the two donkeys on the upper left side are a little close together. If I'm noticing it at this stage, then odds are that it will really bother me when the design is repeated. Such is the law of repeating patterns! I'm going to use my Lasso to select the donkey on the far left, and then I'll click on my "Move" tool to move him over a bit. Then I'm going to erase and redraw the "rope" line between them and clean up the background.

When you are working in channels and want to move or copy an element of your artwork—or make any changes at all—it's necessary to select the channels that you want to be affected. For instance, if I'm going to move the donkey with the yellow basket on his back and part of the background, I will need to select all of my channels except the blue one (since there is no blue in that donkey). You can select more than one channel at a time by holding down the "Shift" key, and then you can move, copy, or paste the lines or colors that these channels make up in any selected area. You can also scale, flip, or otherwise transform whatever you have selected (*see fig. 12*).

⑬ CROP YOUR PATTERN BLOCK

Once you feel you have a good starting place for beginning to build a "pattern block," go ahead and save your file. Remember, a pattern block is the area of artwork that will be

FIG 11 Try new colors for background channel.

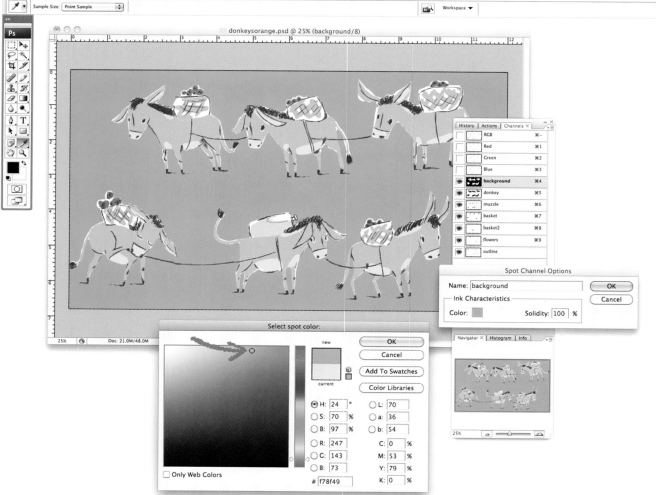

repeated to create the overall design. It can be repeated in several different ways to create different overall effects. Most print-on-demand sites offer their users the same basic options for laying out the block: basic repeat (where the design is repeated in a gridlike pattern), or half-drop, half-brick, or mirror (where the design is staggered, offset, or even flipped to create variation in the final design).

Before uploading your files to the company printing your work, you will want to crop your design so that your pattern block, when repeated horizontally and vertically, will be the same distance from its neighboring pattern block. Use the Cropping tool to select the area you want to preserve. When you release your cursor, you will see handles appear; when pulled, these will allow you to "crop" your image along any of its edges. The area that becomes darkened is the area that you are removing.

The "rulers" along the top and left edges of the screen are helpful tools to make sure spacing is even. And remember, if you make a mistake, you can always select Undo from the "Edit" menu.

⑭ PREPARE YOUR DESIGN FOR UPLOADING

Now you're ready to prepare your file for uploading. First, you'll need to save this file as your master. It's important to hang on to this master file with all your channels still active and your sketch still underneath, so that you can go back later and play with more color options or make any other changes or edits to your artwork. Note, however, that this master file does not get uploaded for printing; it's for your own digital records.

Once the master is saved, you will need to create a copy of the file from the master and give it a new name. Using this

FIG 12 Before moving or cropping, select all channels in that area.

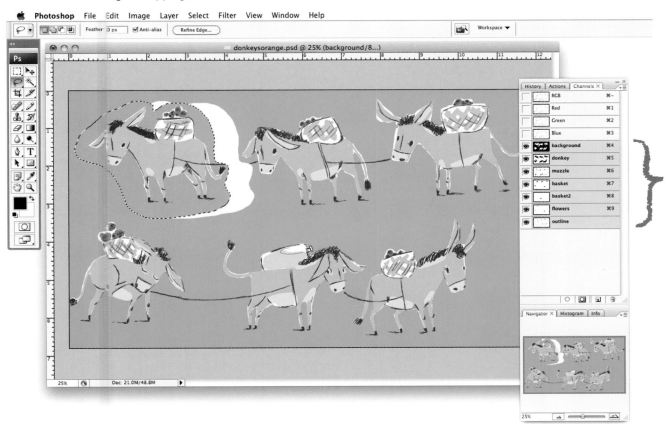

new file, erase the sketch or photo that is underneath all of the channels. (If you try to print fabric using the file that has the sketch or photo underneath, it will peek through!) To delete the underlying sketch, select (and make visible) your RGB channels, then go to your menu bar, click on Select > All, and hit your Delete button (or go to Edit > Clear).

You will also need to change the solidity of all of your spot channels to 100%. You can skip this step if you like the way the colors look as they overlap, but for strong, clear colors and clean edges, you'll want to change the solidity of each channel. You can do this by clicking on the number in the box next to "solidity" in your spot channel window and typing in 100%.

Next, you'll want to "merge" the rest of your channels. You can do this by selecting all of the channels (clicking on each while holding down the "Shift" key). Then click on the small icon in the upper right-hand corner of your channels window to reveal the drop-down menu, and select Merge Spot Channels (see fig. 13).

Now you're ready to save your file as a JPEG and upload it.

⑮ UPLOAD FILE

Once you have saved your file as a JPEG, follow the instructions for uploading your file on the website where it will be printed (see fig. 14). Once the file is uploaded, you will most likely be presented with layout options for repeating the pattern (see fig. 15). If you're noticing too much or too little space between your "blocks," you can go back to your JPEG and recrop the artwork as needed.

FIG 13 Merge spot channels.

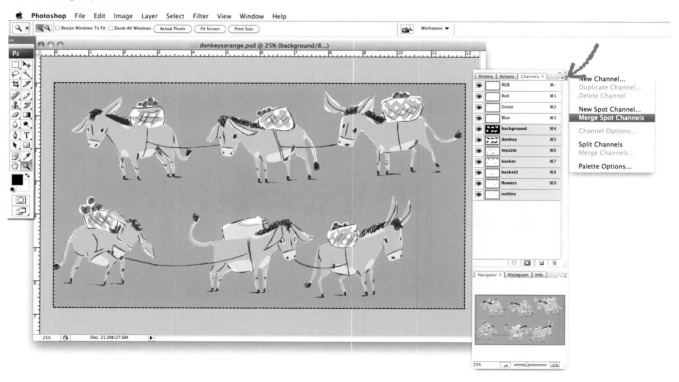

FIG 14 Upload file.

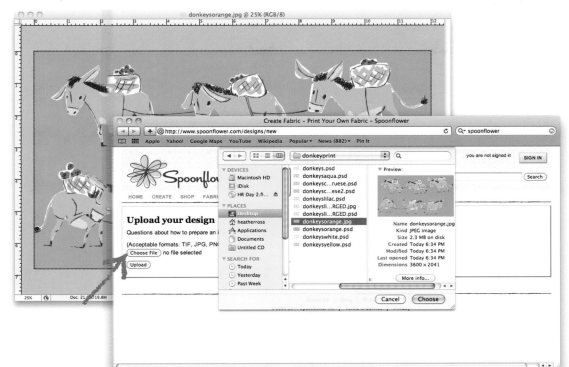

FIG 15 Select pattern repeat.

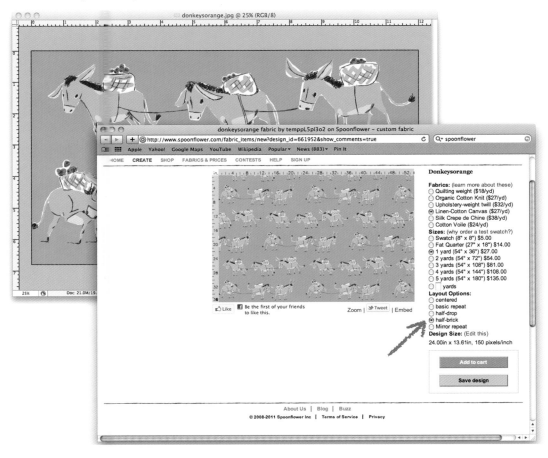

PART THREE

RESOURCES

INDEX OF DIGITAL ART FILES

The disc that comes with this book includes digital artwork in two folders: The artwork in Folder A is meant to be used to make the projects in this book, and the artwork in Folder B is for general crafting and personal use. The index on the following pages includes a thumbnail image of each piece of art that appears on the disc.

FOLDER A: PRINTS FOR PROJECTS

The files in this folder have been specifically formatted for use with the projects in this book and require no alterations on your part. Some projects, such as the Princess and the Pea Wall Hanging on page 65, only have one artwork option available on the disc, while others, such as the Customized Wallpaper on page 23, have several options from which to choose. The first thumbnail image in each row in the index is the artwork that was used in the photographed project—the remainder of thumbnails in the row are the alternate artwork options. The artwork is organized by project; when you're ready to download the file from the disc, simply open the folder for the project you're making, and select the print you want to use. In most cases, the file will be a PDF, and in a few cases (such as the Personalized Notepads on page 51 and the Stationery Suite on page 27), you will have the option to edit the text in the PDF.

FOLDER B: ADDITIONAL HEATHER ROSS PRINTS

This folder contains a selection of my all-time favorite repeating designs. The PDFs are ideal for printing out at home on 8½" x 11" (or A4) sheets of paper and using in any crafty way you can imagine. We have also included all of the designs as JPEGs, which are better suited for uploading to print-on-demand sites when printing fabric yardage or wallpaper.

FOLDER A: PRINTS FOR PROJECTS

SNOW WHITE'S MONOGRAMMED DISHTOWELS (page 19)

Shown in Snow White Dishtowels (each letter of the alphabet is available)

FABRIC-COVERED BAMBOO TRAY (page 21)

Shown in Frog Meadow, *Cream*

CUSTOMIZED WALLPAPER (page 23)

Shown in Unicorns, *Orange*

Underwater Sisters, *Cream*

Horses

Frog Prince, *Lime*

Owl and the Pussycat, *Aqua*

STATIONERY SUITE (page 27)

Shown in Dream Bike

Beach Day

Newspaper Boats

Dogs

Buses

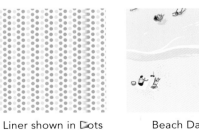   Dogs Buses

Liner shown in Dots

Beach Day

Newspaper Boats

Dogs

Buses

TODDLER DUVET COVER AND PILLOWCASE (page 29)

Shown in Race Track   Shown in Car Blobs

LINEN-COTTON NAPKINS (page 33)

Shown in Botanicals, *Primary*

RICE PAPER LANTERNS, NAME IN LIGHTS (page 35)

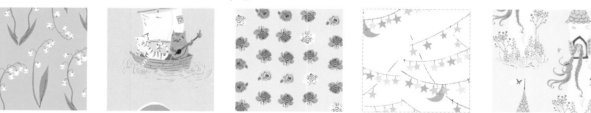

Shown in alternating prints (each letter of the alphabet is available)

RICE PAPER LANTERNS, LARGE LANTERN (page 35)

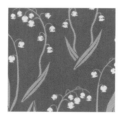    

Shown in Lily, *Plum*   Seagulls   Unicorns, *Lilac*   God's Eye   Daisies and Clover, *Cream*

UNDERWATER SISTERS SHOWER CURTAIN (page 39)

Shown in Underwater Sisters, *Orange*

STITCHED JOURNAL (page 41)

Shown in Snow White, *Gray*

Water Ski Beauties, *Blue*

Seahorses, *Plum*

Dave and Mary's Pond, *Teal*

Daisies and Clover, *Cocoa*

DECOUPAGED CHILDREN'S STORAGE STOOL (page 45)

Shown in Playing Horses

Dream Bike

Underwater Sisters, *Cream*

Owl and the Pussycat, *Aqua*

Buses

PINK ROSE APRON (page 47)

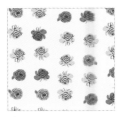
Shown in Repeating Roses, *Pink*

PERSONALIZED NOTEPADS (page 51)

Shown in Underwater Sisters

Snow White, *Laundry*

Princess and the Pea

Becoming Frog

Clothespin Dolls

SUMMER CRICKETS NIGHTGOWN (page 53)

Shown in Crickets

Nightgown Front

Nightgown Back

(MY) HOUSE OF CARDS (page 57)

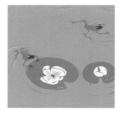

Dave and Mary's
Pond, *Light Green*

Frog Prince, *Purple*

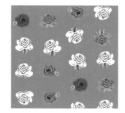

Underwater Sisters,
Purple

Repeating Roses,
Mossy

Underwater Sisters,
Cream

Seahorses, *Sunset*

Swan Lake, *Mud*

Unicorns, *Orange*

Buses

Template

WATER-SKI BEAUTIES VOILE SARONG (page 61)

Shown in Water Ski Beauties, Blue

VOTIVE HOLDERS (page 63)

Shown in Hanging
Stars, *Purple*

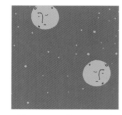

Shown in Stars and
Moons, *Purple*

Shown in
Moons, *Purple*

Shown in Moons,
Gold

PRINCESS AND THE PEA WALL HANGING (page 65)

Shown in Princess and the Pea

FABRIC-BOUND SKETCHBOOK (page 67)

Cover shown in
Wildflowers

Swan Lake, *Mud*

Mermaids

Frog Meadow,
Green

Matroyshka, *Pink*

Endpapers shown in
Playing Horses

Ugly Duckling,
Pink

Seahorses, *Vintage*

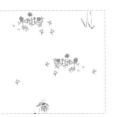

Daisies and Clover,
Cream

Matroyshka,
Flowers

VINYL-COVERED TABLECLOTH (page 70)

Shown in Botanicals,
Pink

WRAPPED GIFTS (page 72)

Clothespin Dolls

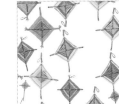

God's Eye

Macaroni Necklace

Newspaper Boats,
Pink

Spools

Newspaper Boats,
Yellow

Hang tags

B FOLDER B: ADDITIONAL HEATHER ROSS PRINTS

  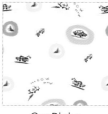 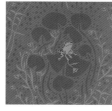

Mermaids   Octopus   Race Track   Car Blobs   Frog Prince, *Purple*

Horses   Beach Day   Swim Class   Princess and the Pea   Lily, *Orange*

Ugly Duckling, *Blue*   Swan Lake, *Blue*   Owl and the Pussycat, *Purple*   Moons, *Yellow*   Becoming Frog

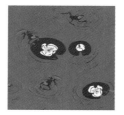    

Dave and Mary's Pond, *Dark Green*   Mushrooms   Clothespin Dolls   Buses   Playing Horses

Matroyshka, *Pink*

Matroyshka, *Flowers*

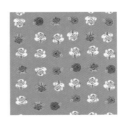

Sleeping Beauty

Repeating Roses, *Mossy*

Dream Bike

Dots

Snow White, *Gray*

Snow White, *Laundry*

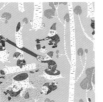

Dogs

Wildflowers

Unicorns, *Green*

Rapunzel

BASIC SEWING REFRESHER

The sewing projects in this book are super easy and are ideal for those who are new to sewing. Presented here is a little refresher course; for additional resources on learning how to sew, check the Recommended Reading list on page 111.

LEARNING TO USE YOUR MACHINE

Once you have bought a machine, refer to its manual to learn how to it set up. Learning to thread it properly is key: Every home-sewing machine uses a variation of the same basic threading system, but each one is slightly different. When my machine is not stitching well, I immediately check to see that both the bobbin thread and needle thread are properly set. If they aren't, that's usually the source of the problem.

After you've mastered threading your machine and wound a few bobbins, learn to use the tension settings: Use different colors for your bobbin thread and needle thread, and stitch a few inches. Can you see your bobbin thread coming through on the side you are stitching? If so, the needle thread tension is too tight, or the bobbin tension is too loose. If, instead, you can see the needle thread on the bottom layer of fabric, the needle thread is too loose, or the bobbin tension is too tight. When the tension is properly adjusted, the two threads will make a tiny knot between the two fabric layers. Also experiment with zigzag stitches and stitch width, and try sewing a few practice buttonholes (see page 108).

PREPARING FABRIC FOR SEWING

When sewing, it's crucial to work with fabric that's "square." That means, in the case of woven fabric, that the vertical warp threads run at a true 90-degree angle to the horizontal weft threads—just as the fabric was originally woven on the loom. But sometimes later steps in the manufacturing process (like stretching the fabric for printing or just incorrectly winding the finished fabric on the bolt) may cause what was originally square fabric to get out of square. As a result, unless you square up the fabric again before sewing it and unless you position your pattern pieces correctly with the straight (squared) grain of the fabric, your project will also be out of square.

Ask the salesperson to cut the yardage either by tearing it (meaning to actually rip it across its width, which gives you a very straight edge since the rip follows a crosswise weft thread in the fabric's weave) or by "pulling a thread" (meaning to pull out a single weft thread, leaving a tiny, but visible, empty space in the fabric's weave to serve as a cutting guide). Both cutting methods will give you a square cut, even if sometimes the cut fabric still looks out of square. Square fabric that just looks out of square is easily remedied by "trueing" it.

FABRIC CUT SQUARE AND OFF-SQUARE

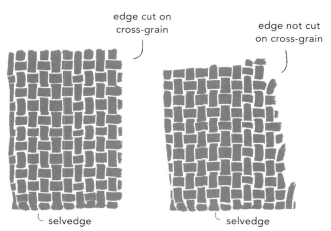

edge cut on cross-grain

edge not cut on cross-grain

selvedge · selvedge

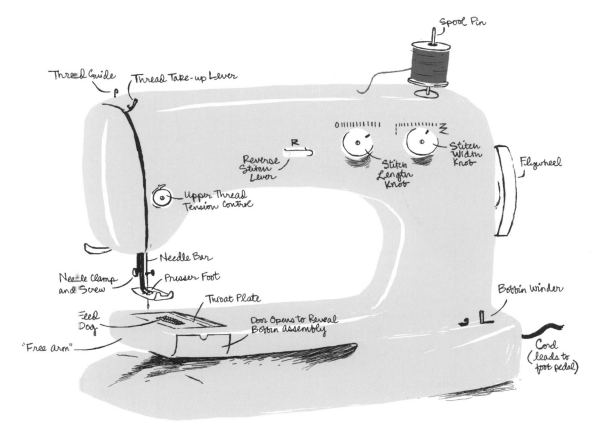

Spool Pin

Thread Guide Thread Take-up Lever

Reverse Stitch Lever

R

Stitch Length Knob

Stitch Width Knob

Flywheel

Upper Thread Tension Control

Needle Bar

Needle Clamp and Screw

Presser Foot

Feed Dog

Throat Plate

Door Opens to Reveal Bobbin assembly

"Free arm"

Bobbin Winder

Cord (leads to foot pedal)

TRUEING YOUR FABRIC

The process of trueing woven fabric involves washing, drying, and pressing it to make sure that all its horizontal and vertical threads line up perfectly, as they did when the fabric was originally woven. Trueing the fabric returns it to its original square state and should always be done before cutting pattern pieces from it. An added benefit of trueing is that it preshrinks the fabric. (Before you start trueing your fabric, if it was not cut correctly at the fabric store by either ripping it on the cross-grain or pulling a cross-grain thread, as explained above, do this now on both of the fabric's cut ends.)

To true your fabric, first wash and dry it according to the manufacturer's instructions. Press the washed and dried fabric, lay it flat, and smooth it from the center toward the selvedges and cut edges. Next, fold the fabric across its width, and smooth it out until its cut edges match (the cut edges will match exactly only if your fabric was torn or cut on the straight grain), as shown in the drawing at right. Put a few pins into the fabric to

keep the folded layers from slipping, and press the squared fabric again, so it's ready for cutting.

While trueing the fabric may seem like a lot of work, it makes a world of difference in the way your finished project looks and feels.

Smooth fabric away from folded edge until both cut edges match, and press fabric again.

STITCHES YOU'LL NEED

You will only need two stitches to make the projects in this book: straight stitch and zigzag stitch. (Note that these stitches are machine stitches, not hand stitches.)

straight stitch

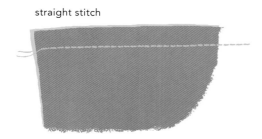

Straight Stitch

A straight stitch is the stitch most commonly used for sewing seams. On most sewing machines, you can adjust the stitch's length, and although most sewing calls for a regular stitch length (2.5–3 mm, or 10–12 stitches per inch [2.5 cm] for mid-weight fabrics), some project directions will call for a shorter or longer stitch length. Unless otherwise noted, the width of the seams for the sewing projects in this book is ½" (1.3 cm). To secure each straight-stitch seam, unless noted otherwise, it's a good idea to begin and end it by back-tacking (sewing in reverse) or lockstitching (sewing with the stitch length set to zero) for a few stitches.

zigzag stitch

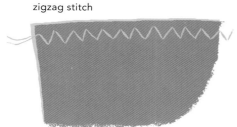

Zigzag Stitch

Most home-sewing machines made in the last fifty years feature a stitch-width adjustment lever. By adjusting the stitch's width, you can make your needle move to the right and left as it sews, either subtly or dramatically, depending on how wide and long you set the stitch to be. This stitch is aptly named the zigzag stitch. Unlike a straight stitch, a zigzag stitch, even a very narrow one, has some give to it—that is, it stretches a little when pulled from end to end.

MAKING BUTTONHOLES

Buttonholes are made by sewing a rectangle of zigzag stitches—two narrow-zigzag vertical "legs," capped top and bottom by a wide-zigzag horizontal bar—to create a reinforced area in the fabric that can be slit to allow a button to pass through.

To make a buttonhole, first determine how large an opening your button needs: Cut a small strip of paper, about 4" (10.2 cm) long x ¼"(6 mm) wide. Wrap the strip around the button's widest part, grasping the paper firmly where its two edges meet; pencil-mark this point; and remove the button. Keeping the paper strip folded, flatten it, and measure and record the length from fold to pencil mark.

With a water-soluble fabric-marking pen, mark an X on the fabric where you want to place your buttonhole, then draw a centered vertical line through each X the length of your button measurement.

Attach the buttonhole foot to your machine. This foot has ruled marks on it, so you can measure and sew the exact length needed for your marked buttonhole. Always practice making a few buttonholes on scrap fabric before sewing on your actual garment, and cut one of the practice buttonholes open to make sure it fits your button.

Many machines have automatic buttonhole settings. If yours doesn't, attach the machine's buttonhole foot, and follow the steps below to manually machine-sew a buttonhole.

① Sew Top Horizontal Bar
(Settings: *Machine's adjustable needle bar: center; stitch length: just above zero; stitch width: widest possible*)

Place the fabric under the buttonhole foot, with the needle positioned at the top end of the marked buttonhole line. Sew a few stitches, which will be wide, almost completely horizontal stitches, creating a horizontal "bar" for the top of the buttonhole. Stop stitching at the far left side of the bar, with the needle down in the fabric.

② Sew Left Leg
(Settings: *Needle bar: far left; stitch length: almost zero; stitch width: medium*)

Stitch down the marked line to the bottom, stopping at the far left, with the needle down in the fabric.

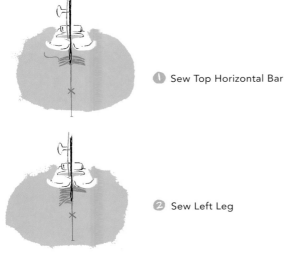

① Sew Top Horizontal Bar

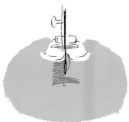

② Sew Left Leg

③ Sew Bottom Horizontal Bar

④ Sew Right Leg

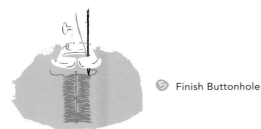

⑤ Finish Buttonhole

③ **Sew Bottom Horizontal Bar**

(Settings: *Needle bar: center; stitch length: almost zero; stitch width: widest possible*)

Sew a few stitches, creating the bottom horizontal bar. Stop stitching at the far right, with the needle down in the fabric.

④ **Sew Right Leg**

(Settings: *Needle bar: center; stitch length: almost zero; stitch width: medium*)

Sew in reverse back up the buttonhole's length to the beginning stitches.

⑤ **Finish the Buttonhole**

(Setting: *Stitch width: zero*)

Set the stitch length to zero and take a couple of stitches in place. Then pull the top thread to the wrong side and knot off with the bobbin thread. To open the buttonhole, use a seam ripper, small scissors, or buttonhole cutter to cut the fabric between the two stitching rows, being careful not to cut the stitches themselves.

SEWING ON BUTTONS

Sew buttons on by hand with a hand-sewing needle and cotton or poly-cotton thread that matches your button (not the fabric), unless you want to add interest by using a contrasting thread.

① Mark your button placements: After cutting your sewn buttonholes open, lay the garment flat, with the buttonhole placket positioned over where you want the buttons to go. Push the tip of a water-soluble fabric-marking pen through the center of each open buttonhole, making a small button-placement mark on the fabric beneath. Using a single, knotted strand of thread and working on the right side, make a small stitch in the same spot you marked.

② Sew in and out of the holes in the button in an X pattern until the button is secure. Your last stitch should come through the fabric from the back, ending between the button and the fabric's right side.

③ Then wrap the thread around the sewn thread shank below the button several times, pulling all of the threads together. Push the needle through the shank and knot off several times. Clip thread tails.

SOURCES FOR SUPPLIES

The projects in this book require a combination of new technologies and tools along with age-old crafting supplies. I realize, however, that computer systems can vary, so I've tried to keep the basic requirements as simple as possible, keeping in mind that cost and accessibility will be a limitation for many. Below is a list of the brands and resources I prefer. For more information on necessary system requirements and alternate technology options, see page 11.

COMPUTER SOFTWARE AND TOOLS

Adobe Reader
http://get.adobe.com/reader/otherversions/
A free program needed to use the files on the disc.

Adobe Photoshop
www.adobe.com/products/photoshop
In order to create your own digital designs (see page 78), you will need Adobe Photoshop CS5.

Wacom Digitizer and Stylus
www.wacom.com/en/products/intuos.aspx
The stylus is used in place of a mouse; it is held like a pen and used to "draw" on the digitizer tablet.

GENERAL CRAFTING SUPPLIES

Most of the materials and supplies used to make the projects in this book can be found at retailers nationwide, such as:

A.C. Moore www.acmoore.com

Dick Blick Art Materials www.dickblick.com

Hobby Lobby www.hobbylobby.com

Jo-Ann www.joann.com

Michael's www.michaels.com

Pearl www.pearlpaint.com

Save-on-Crafts www.save-on-crafts.com

If you cannot find a specific item, try these online resources:

Bamboo Tray:
www.muji.us/store/wooden-tray-2-ash-wood-square.html

Child's Wooden Storage Stool:
www.amazon.com/Gift-Mark-Childrens-Stool-Storage/dp/B001AMR690

Fabrics and Notions:
www.spoonflower.com (for print-on-demand fabric)
www.purlsoho.com (for fabric, pom-pom fringe, and grommets)
www.sewzannesfabrics.com (for fold-over elastic)

Lamp Equipment:
www.lampshop.com/ (for wire uno lampshade rings)
www.partylights.com (for string bulb lights on a 10-foot [3-meter] cord)

Paper and Boards:
www.moleskine.com (for Moleskine sketchbooks)
www.americanframe.com (for archival mounting board)
www.uline.com (for chipboard)
www.paper-source.com (for rice paper, vellum, and A6 notecards and envelopes)

Tapes and Adhesives:
www.pearlpaint.com (double-coated tape)
www.lineco.com (linen book-binding tape, padding compound, and neutral pH adhesive)

Wallpaper:
www.designyourwallcovering.com (for print-on-demand wallpaper)

RECOMMENDED READING

EDUCATIONAL

Adobe Photoshop for Textile Design: For Adobe Photoshop CS3, by Frederick L. Chipkin
This book offers in-depth information about how to use Photoshop to create textile designs.

Digital Textile Design (Portfolio Skills: Fashion and Textiles), by Melanie Bowles and Ceri Isaac
This book offers excellent instruction for those who are especially interested in turning their artwork and photographs into digitally printed fabrics.

Mastering the Art of Fabric Printing and Design, by Laurie Wisbrun
This book offers an introduction to the field of fabric design and some great interviews with modern-day textile designers. Loads of inspiring tips!

Printing by Hand: A Modern Guide to Printing with Handmade Stamps, Stencils, and Silk Screens, by Lena Corwin
Lena Corwin is one of my favorite designers working today. Her book will inspire you to turn your kitchen table into a printing studio.

Singer Complete Photo Guide to Sewing (Revised + Expanded Edition), by the editors of Creative Publishing
This book offers very simple visual instructions, perfect for beginning sewists, and is a great reference book for more seasoned sewists.

www.tempaperdesigns.com
Provides great online tutorials for hanging peel-and-stick wallpaper.

INSPIRATIONAL

Vera: The Art and Life of an Icon, by Susan Seid
Vera Neumann's textiles inspired me to become an artist. This book tells the story of her career trajectory and business model, which is also the story of a woman creating a successful business and brand at a time when this was not as common as it is today.

Textile Designs: Two Hundred Years of European and American Patterns Organized by Motif, Style, Color, Layout, and Period, by Susan Meller and Joost Elffers
An encyclopedia of fabric design, with page after page of beautiful prints. If you own just own reference book about fabric design, this should be it!

V&A Pattern: Slipcased Sets, by V&A Publications
The Victoria and Albert museum in London holds the finest library of textile designs in the world. In this DVD/book set (which is part of what inspired this book), V&A designs are available as digital files.

TEAR-OUT SHEETS PRINTED WITH HEATHER ROSS DESIGNS

And finally, just for fun, here are a few pages of some of my favorite prints for you to use as you please. You can photocopy the prints or tear them out along the perforation and use them for all sorts of crafts, such as origami, gift wrap, scrapbooking, envelope liners, a pretty paper airplane, mobiles, or decoupage (to name a few).

ACKNOWLEDGMENTS

This book, which I wrote while pregnant at the age of forty, would not have been possible without the help of my wonderful assistant, Vera McLaughlin. Vera is like sunshine with feet—not even the most daunting tasks can challenge her ever-happy mood and can-do attitude (even when I'm asking her to do things like "Please learn how to hang wallpaper by tomorrow").

During the photo shoot, I spent some long, rainy days in the middle of the woods with Vera, John Gruen (our photographer), and Alex Harney (John's assistant), as well as a very smelly, muddy dog, and biting insects. We all stayed together in a big haunted house that was under construction, and there were limited dining options, yet somehow we managed to have a lot of fun. This says a great deal about the personalities and professional abilities of John and Alex, both of whom I'm very pleased to call my friends. I spent a lot of time during this project wondering if they would ever agree to go anywhere with me again. Pauline Wall came and cooked for us and even tried to wash the dog, which didn't work out as well as her lovely meals, but that wasn't her fault.

Thanks go to my most generous and well-appointed neighbors—Chuck and Nancy Fredericks and the Robbins Family—for introducing me to their most inspirational and perfect corner of the Catskills, as well as for providing the loveliest accommodations and some spectacular settings in which to take photographs. Chuck, if the black flies hadn't chased us away screaming, your jewel of a hermitage would have landed on the cover, I swear. I'll be back.

My beautiful friend Paisley Gregg once again braved country roads to come and spend a day being photographed. Paisley gets prettier and more adventurous with every passing year, which is lucky for me. STC Craft's own Liana Allday (who is also my editor) put down her red pen for a day to do the same—and yes, you have seen her before in the pages of other STC books. As I tell her every time I ask her to get in front of the camera: With great attractiveness comes great responsibility.

Liana and I agonized together over the design chapter in this book and whether or not it would "work." I invited her to my studio to test the Photoshop tutorial herself, and when I saw how excited she was with her finished design, I knew it would be my favorite chapter. Her enthusiasm and passion for all things crafty is a big part of why the books that come from STC Craft are so beautiful and inspirational.

There comes a happy point in any career when others start to fight the creative fights for you. When this happens, the world suddenly becomes a much easier place to navigate. In my case, those people are my agent, Steven Malk, and the director of STC Craft, Melanie Falick. Steven saw the potential for a project like this one, even though he specializes in other markets, and he and Melanie both worked hard to make sure it would be the book I wanted it to be, despite it being an arguably unproven and untested format. Melanie has been a true teacher and friend these past five years. If anyone out there actually thinks it's possible to publish books without an editor, then they have never worked with a great one.

One of the best parts about this project has been getting to work with my friend Brooke Hellewell Reynolds on the graphic design. Brooke moved across the country a few years ago, and I miss her. She's a wonderful graphic designer and I've learned a lot from her about book design, crafting, and juggling babies with work.

As always, thanks to my husband, TC Fleming, my sister, Christine Danner, my dear friend Denyse Schmidt, and my father, Hank Ross. Behind any moderately successful entrepreneur there must be someone who pays the light bill, holds the tissue box, nods knowingly, and brags about you to anyone who will listen. Without you four, I would be quite in the dark.

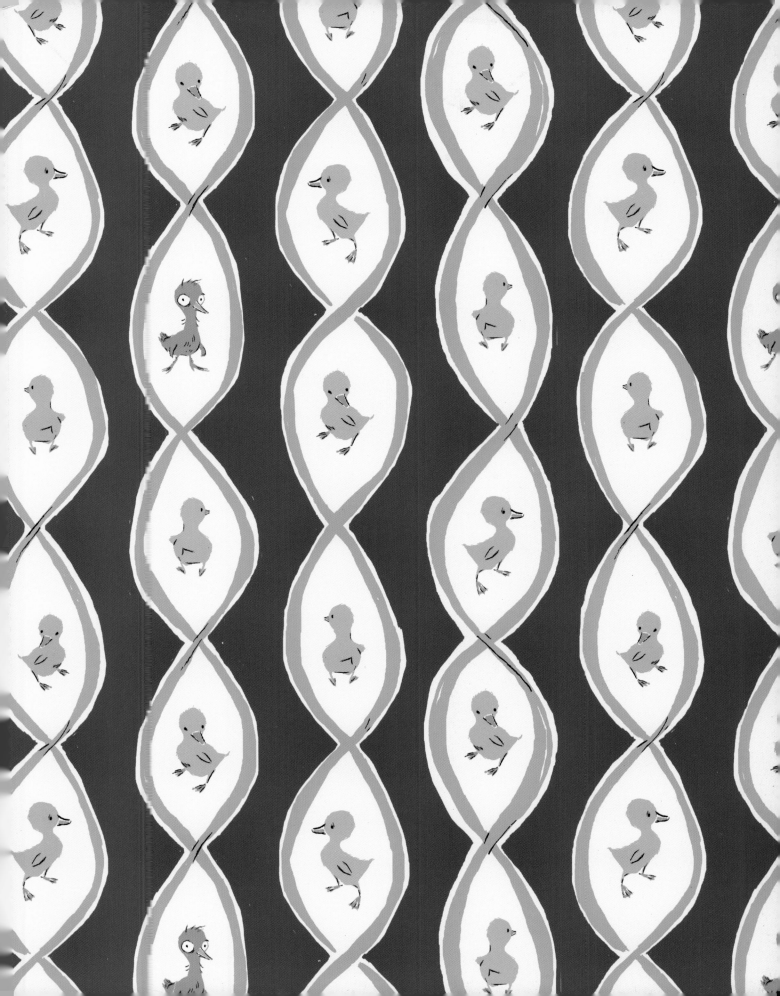

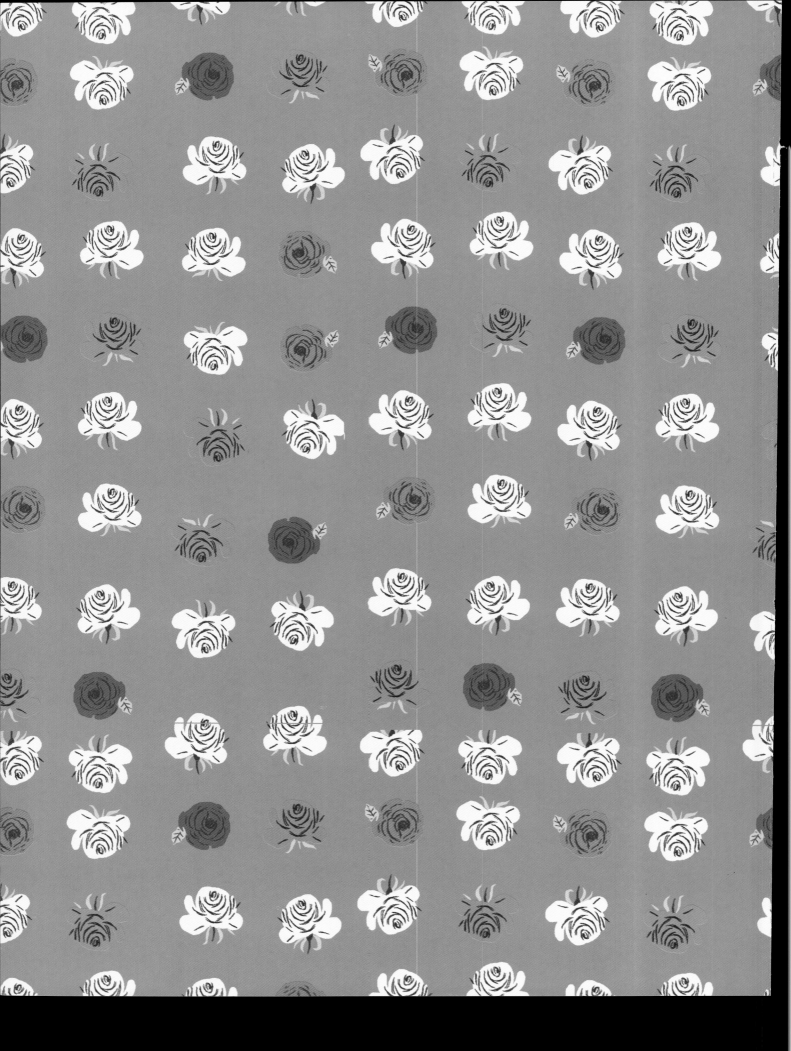

they were
a merry
band of brothers,
without a mother
to mind them.